THOMAS JEFFERSON
[From the painting by Gilbert Stuart, owned by T. Jefferson Coolidge, Esq.]

THE
JEFFERSONIAN SYSTEM

1801–1811

BY

EDWARD CHANNING, Ph.D.
PROFESSOR OF HISTORY, HARVARD UNIVERSITY

WITH MAPS

GREENWOOD PRESS, PUBLISHERS
NEW YORK

Originally published in 1906
by Harper & Brothers

First Greenwood Reprinting 1969

Library of Congress Catalogue Card Number 69-13855

PRINTED IN UNITED STATES OF AMERICA

CONTENTS

x CONTENTS

MAPS

EDITOR'S INTRODUCTION

THE title of *The Jeffersonian System*, chosen for this volume, with the title of its predecessor, Bassett's *Federalist System*, suggests two rival, and in some respects opposed, groups of political principles and methods of carrying on both the federal and the state governments. Nevertheless, however different in point of view, the problems of Jefferson and Madison were, with the one great exception of the Louisiana purchase, substantially the same as those of Washington and Adams.

The personality of Thomas Jefferson is in many ways the dominant note in the period from 1801 to 1811. In chapters i. and ii. Professor Channing brings out how far Jefferson supposed himself to be inaugurating a new era, and in what respects he tried to undo or to supplant the work of his predecessors. After a brief chapter (iii.) on the Tripolitan War follows, in chapters iv., v., and vi., a systematic account of the conditions, progress, and results of the annexation of Louisiana, to which a convenient introduction may be found in Thwaites's *France in America*, chapter xviii. In chapter vii. the exploration of the west is taken up at a point where that important subject was left by McLaughlin's

Confederation and Constitution, chapter viii., and by
Bassett's *Federalist System*, chapter xiii. Chapter
viii. is on the prohibition of the slave-trade. Chapters ix. and x. deal with the political controversies
centring about the impeachment of Justice Chase
and the defection of John Randolph on the Yazoo
question.

Chapters xi. and xii. again resume the thread of our
frontier relations in West Florida and in Texas, including Burr's conspiracy. Thereafter the main
subject of the book is the complications arising from
the renewal of the war in Europe in 1803, and the
consequent aggressions upon the neutral trade of
the United States, including the *Chesapeake-Leopard*
affair, the decrees and orders in council, the embargo and non-intercourse. Chapter xx., on the ap-
proaching war with Great Britain, may be compared
with chapters i. and ii. of Babcock's *Rise of American Nationality* (vol. XIII.), which show the results
of the causes here suggested.

In the *American Nation* series this volume em-
phasizes the innate tendency to expansion of territory, of which Louisiana, West Florida, and Oregon
were all examples. The special and successful purpose of the author is to make clear how it was possible for the nation to expand in territory and in
spirit, and for the federal government to gain consequence and authority, while at the same time the
government was growing more democratic: it is a
study in imperial democracy.

AUTHOR'S PREFACE

JEFFERSON'S first administration has always had a great attraction for the writer of the present volume. At one time, indeed, he thought of making it the subject of a prolonged investigation. From that design he was turned by the sight of some advanced sheets of Henry Adams's work on the early Republican administrations. In no way can the admiration for that notable book be better shown than by making it the foundation of the following sketch. In this place, therefore, a general reference is made to Henry Adams's masterpiece. In the following pages only those portions of it will be cited which contain matter inaccessible to the present writer. In addition to Mr. Adams's *History* and his *Gallatin,* recourse has been had to the well-known collections of documents and letters and to the more important material published since the close of Mr. Adams's research. References to these works will be found in the foot-notes of the pages. At the end of the volume is a critical estimate of some of them.

EDWARD CHANNING.

THE
JEFFERSONIAN SYSTEM

THE
JEFFERSONIAN SYSTEM

CHAPTER I

ORGANIZATION OF JEFFERSON'S ADMINISTRATION

(1801–1805)

THE revolution of 1800 was accomplished: the Federalists had fallen, the Republicans were supreme. It was now the time to take possession of the government and to seize upon the spoils of victory. At twelve o'clock, March 4, 1801, Thomas Jefferson, the newly elected president, left his lodgings and walked across the square to the partly finished Capitol. In this progress he was accompanied by the secretaries of the navy and treasury, who represented the outgoing administration, some notable personages, and a few political friends, while the militia from the neighborhood furnished an escort. As he ascended the steps of the Capitol, a discharge of artillery was made—to the admiration, no doubt, of the assembled population of the infant city of Washington.[1] Entering the Senate chamber, he took the vice-president's chair. On one side was Aaron Burr, the new vice-president; on the other was John Marshall, the new chief-justice of the supreme court of the United States. It was an interesting group; doubly interesting, indeed, because probably in the whole country there could not have been found three men who more thoroughly detested and distrusted one another than Thomas Jefferson, John Marshall, and Aaron Burr.

President Jefferson was now fifty-eight years of age. He was tall—six feet, two inches and a half in height—with a red, freckled face and a loose, shackling air. He appeared to an English observer to resemble a large-boned farmer rather than the chief magistrate of a great nation. In manner he was shy and stiff, and sat cornerwise on his chair, with one shoulder elevated high above the other. One would scarcely have thought that this loose-jointed man was the most astute political leader then living in the United States. Jefferson, in truth, was an idealist who was in politics from a sincere desire to save the nation from those whom he termed monocrats and monopolists. He was a brilliant conversationalist and deeply interested in original scientific investigations. In the spring of 1801, when he was carrying on the government of the United States

---

[1] Adams, *United States*, I., 185; McMaster, *United States*, II., 533, gives extracts from the *Aurora* of March 11, 1801, describing the "instalment."

almost single-handed, he could not put away his
longing for scientific debate. On March 17 of that
year he wrote to Philip Mazzei, telling him of the
new administration and also of certain seeds which
he had sent him. These were the seeds of the
cymbling (*Cucurbita vermeosa*) and of the squash
(*Cucurbita melopipo*). Of these, Jefferson thought
that the squash was "the best tasted," but by plant-
ing the cymbling and the pumpkin near together
one might produce the perfect equivalent of the
squash—at least so he wrote. This epistle would
seem to contain no incriminating matter, but, re-
membering the indiscretion of his correspondent on
an earlier occasion,[1] he closed with the statement
that he added no signature because of the perils by
land and by sea to which the letter might be exposed.

John Marshall was also a Virginian, but he held
Jefferson's political theories in utter detestation.
Simpler in manner even than the Republican president, the Federalist chief-justice had a mind as
coldly logical as Jefferson's was warmly idealistic.
He believed the political morals of the new president
to be most impure, while Jefferson, on his part,
regarded the chief-justice as a gloomy malignant
who would never forego the opportunity to satisfy
his revengeful appetite on the quivering flesh of his
victim. It would have been interesting to have
heard what Marshall said to himself as he held out
the Bible on which Jefferson swore to "preserve,

[1] See Bassett, *Federalist System* (*Am. Nation*, XI.), chap. ix.

protect, and defend the Constitution of the United States."

The organization of the new government was a matter of considerable difficulty and occupied a good deal of time. Madison was the designated secretary of state; but at the moment he was busy with his private affairs and could not enter upon the discharge of his official duties. Albert Gallatin was likewise designated as secretary of the treasury, but his confirmation by the existing Senate was so doubtful that it was thought best to defer his appointment until after the Senate had adjourned, in the expectation that the new Senate, which would meet for the first time in the following December, would contain a Republican majority. For some months Jefferson, with Dexter and Stoddert, two members of Adams's cabinet, administered the government as well as they could. In the summer-time Jefferson retired to Monticello to avoid the enervating influences of the Washington climate, and for two months the government carried on itself. It speaks well for the Federalist organization that everything did not go to pieces in this interval. When the cooler weather came in the autumn, the president gathered his advisers about him and set vigorously to work to reform the laws, the finances, and the civil service. Besides Madison and Gallatin, General Dearborn, of Massachusetts, and Levi Lincoln of the same state, filled the offices of secretary of war and attorney-general, while Gideon Granger, of Connecticut, per-

formed the duties of postmaster-general. The position of secretary of the navy was so hard to fill that
at one time Jefferson laughingly suggested he might
have to advertise for candidates. In time, however, Robert Smith, of Maryland, brother of General
Samuel Smith, was appointed to the vacant place,
and the list of Jefferson's official advisers was complete. Of these, Madison and Gallatin were the
most prominent and the ablest, but Lincoln's opinion was steadily sought and always respected, although not always followed.

James Madison, Virginia born, like Jefferson and
Marshall, enjoyed the advantage of having attended
the College of New Jersey at Princeton. Although
he was ten years younger than Jefferson, he had been
long in political life. He had striven earnestly for
the establishment of a strong national government
in the Federal convention, and his weighty arguments had carried the day against George Mason
and Patrick Henry in the Virginia ratifying convention.[1] With Hamilton and Jay, he had written
the *Federalist*. He had been a member of the House
of Representatives in the first Congress under the
Constitution, and had played a prominent part in
the organization of the new fabric. Then he fell
under the influence of Jefferson, and became his
most trusted adviser and lieutenant. Although he
was dry and formal in manner and weak in appear-

[1] See McLaughlin, *Confederation and Constitution* (*Am. Nation*,
X.), chap. xvii.

ance, James Madison had a mind of his own and knew how and when to secure the accomplishment of his purposes. Jefferson's other confidential friend and adviser was Albert Gallatin. He was of Genevan origin, and never overcame his foreign accent; for a year, indeed, he had taught French at Harvard College. Bred to politics and to the leading of men, Gallatin had none of the shyness of Jefferson or the apparent lack of force of Madison, but he was sometimes deficient in tact. He entered public life at about the time of the formation of the Republican party, and must have appeared to Jefferson as one sent from heaven—for he could juggle with figures as well as the best of them, even Alexander Hamilton himself could not more hopelessly tie up a financial problem than this third, foreign-born head of the United States treasury. He was precisely the man the Republicans needed, for most of them were more expert at farming than at figures.[1]

To return to "the instalment," as the *Aurora* termed the inauguration ceremonies, Thomas Jefferson, seated, and in a low voice, read his first inaugural address[2] to his friends and that portion of his fellow-citizens that was assembled before him. With the exception of the Declaration of Independence and the 1796 letter to Mazzei, none of Jefferson's

[1] Adams, *Life of Gallatin;* J. A. Stevens, *Albert Gallatin (Am. Statesmen Series).*
[2] Richardson, *Messages and Papers*, I., 321; Jefferson, *Writings* (Ford's ed.), VIII., 1.

writings have had a greater reputation than this address. The Federalists made fun of its mixed metaphors and grammatical inaccuracies, but those were matters which did not trouble the philosopher of Monticello. Six months later (November, 1801) he wrote to Madison that, where by small grammatical negligences the energy of an idea is condensed or a word can be made to stand for a sentence, he held grammatical rigor in contempt,[1] and, a few months earlier, he had stigmatized Noah Webster as a mere pedagogue of very limited understanding.[2] Jefferson's Republican constituents were quite willing to overlook the small negligences of grammar and to see in his first inaugural the wisdom of the sage. The new president recognized in the great overturn of 1800 a revolution as important and far-reaching in its consequences as that which began in 1775. The revolution, however, was accomplished, and Jefferson's policy was now to conciliate his fellow-countrymen, with the exception of these monarchical Federalists whom nothing but death could change. It was in this spirit that he exclaimed, "We are all Republicans! We are all Federalists!" He then went on to state the principles which should be the creed of our political faith and the "text of civic instruction." It will be well to recount these somewhat more at length.

The sum of good government, Jefferson declared, was that which, while it shall "restrain men from

[1] Jefferson, *Writings* (Ford's ed.), VIII., 108.   [2] *Ibid.*, 80.

injuring one another, shall leave them otherwise
free to regulate their own pursuits of industry and
improvement, and shall not take from the mouth of
labor the bread it has earned." He then stated
these aphorisms: Equal and exact justice to all men;
peace, commerce, and friendship with all nations,
entangling alliances with none; the support of the
state governments in all their rights; the preservation of the general government, in its whole constitutional vigor; a jealous care of the rights of
election by the people; absolute acquiescence in the
decisions of the majority; a well-disciplined militia;
the supremacy of the civil over the military authority; economy in public expense; the honest payment
of all debts; and sacred preservation of the public faith; encouragement of agriculture, and of commerce as its handmaid; the diffusion of information,
and arraignment of all abuses at the bar of public
reason; freedom of religion, freedom of the press,
and freedom of the person; these were the principles
which led to peace, liberty, and safety.

Although Jefferson had said, "We are all Republicans! We are all Federalists!" he very soon came
to a realizing sense of the necessity of encouraging
his supporters and paying pre-election debts[1] by the
gift of offices which could only be made at the expense of those who still called themselves Federalists. He gained some offices by regarding as nul-

[1] See, for example, the case of James Linn as described by
John Randolph in Adams, *Randolph*, 52.

lities those appointments which Adams had made
after the results of the election were known, and
even as late, according to Jefferson, as nine o'clock
in the evening of March 3. The partisanship of
Adams, and, it must be said, of Washington also
in his last years, had filled the offices with Federalists. In 1795, Washington had laid down the general principle that no one should be appointed to
office whose political tenets were adverse to the
measures of the government. To do otherwise, he
thought, would be "a sort of political suicide."[1] A
majority of the voters had now taken the government away from the Federalists and had intrusted
it to the Republicans. Jefferson felt that the revolution of 1800 would not be complete until many,
at least, of the appointive offices were in the hands
of members of that party which had been successful
at the polls; and he would have laid himself open
to the charge of hypocrisy if he had thought otherwise. At first, he proposed to remove those only
who had been guilty of official malconduct and the
attorneys and marshals in the federal courts. The
lopping off of the officers of the courts he justified on
the ground that as all the federal judges were Federalists, the only way to secure a fair hearing for
Republicans was to have the ministerial officers of
the federal courts of that political stripe. With
the exception of this last group of officers, he thought
that no removals should be made on the ground of

[1] Washington, *Writings* (Ford's ed.), XIII., 107.

politics alone.[1] He soon found, however, that such
a small charge of office-holders would not serve as
sufficient encouragement to his own supporters. He
therefore began to make removals for offensive partisanship; but the number of removals made for
purely political reasons was astonishingly small[2] and
not at all commensurate with the wishes of some
of his supporters.[3]

The most interesting of all his removals—most
interesting because it attracted the greatest attention — was that of Elizur Goodrich, collector of
customs at New Haven, Connecticut, who had been
appointed by Adams some two weeks before the
close of his administration. As one of the late ap-
pointees, Goodrich came under the general nullification of Adams's "last appointments." Affairs
in Connecticut were in a peculiar state, if we may
believe the testimony of Gideon Granger and Pierre-
pont Edwards. According to the latter,[4] the Federalists were most systematically organized. The
governor and council, with the corporation of Yale
College, of whom thirteen out of twenty-one were
described as "ecclesiastics," dominated the state.
Yale College, indeed, was violently opposed to the

---

[1] Jefferson, Writings (Ford's ed.), VIII., 10, 32, 37, 47.
[2] See, however, other estimates by J. M. Merriam in Am.
Hist. Assoc., Papers, II., 51, and by C. R. Fish, Civil Service and
Patronage, 42; and in Am. Hist. Assoc., Report, 1889, p. 70.
[3] See, for instance, Dodd, Nathaniel Macon, 168; Gallatin,
Writings (Adams's ed.), I., 130.
[4] Am. Hist. Rev., III., 275.

new order of things, if Theodore Dwight, brother of
Timothy Dwight, its president, may be supposed to
have represented its feelings. In an oration delivered at New Haven, July 7, 1801, he declared that
the great object of Jacobinism, as he denominated
Republicanism, was to destroy every trace of civilization in the world, and to force mankind back into
the savage state. "We have a country," he said,
"governed by blockheads and knaves; . . . our
children are cast into the world from the breast
and forgotten; filial piety is extinguished, and our
surnames, the only mark of distinction among families, are abolished. Can the imagination paint anything more dreadful on this side of hell?" And
he was not alone in his opinions. For on the preceding Fourth of July the voters of Middletown,
Connecticut, drank to the toast, "Thomas Jefferson,
may he receive from his fellow-citizens the reward
of his merit—a halter." The person appointed to
succeed Elizur Goodrich was Samuel Bishop, mayor
of the city of New Haven and holder of several
offices under the state government, whose son, Abraham Bishop,[1] had vigorously advocated the cause of
Republicanism.

The merchants of New Haven protested against
this change in the custom-house, and their protest

[1] See Franklin B. Dexter, "Abraham Bishop," in Mass. Hist.
Soc., *Proceedings*, 1905. It appears from this paper that Bishop
was not permitted to deliver his address on "Political Delusion"
before the literary societies of Yale College as stated on the
title-page of the essay.

gave Jefferson an opportunity to state his policy as
to removals as it appeared to him in the summer of
1801. In this communication he sought to show
that the character and capacity of Samuel Bishop
had been carefully inquired into before the appointment was made. He called attention to the fact
that in the preceding May the Federalist legislature
of Connecticut had appointed Bishop to be chief
judge of the court of common pleas of New Haven
county, and sole judge of the court of probate in
that same county. "Is it possible," he asks, "that
the man to whom the legislature of Connecticut
has recently committed trusts of such difficulty
and magnitude is unfit to be the collector of the
district?" He then takes up the question of the
removal of Goodrich and justifies it on the ground
of its being one of Adams's "last appointments."
Besides, the Republicans, being in the majority, had
a right to some of the offices. If due participation in office is a matter of right, Jefferson asked,
how are vacancies to be obtained, save by removal? "Those by death are few; by resignation,
none."[1]

The machinery of the administration at Washington was bottomed on that of the state governments,
and that, in turn, reflected, in a measure, the system
which had grown up in England itself. In none
of these places—scarcely, indeed, out of China—had
the thought of selecting the holders of public office

[1] Jefferson, *Writings* (Ford's ed.), VIII., 70.

by competitive examination occurred to any one.
To go no further back, President Washington had
picked out his men in consultation with the political
leaders in the different parts of the country; so had
Adams, and so, too, did Jefferson. The advent of
the new administration marked the first change
from one party to another in the national government and the first opportunity for any considerable
change among the office-holders. There was as
much eagerness for office in those days as there is
now; but the isolation of the city of Washington
and the difficulties and dangers incurred in a journey
thither prevented the rush of the hordes of office-
seekers which has been witnessed in more recent
times. Importunity generally took the form of
letters instead of personal solicitation. Jefferson's
mail was weighted down with applications and letters of recommendation, and pressure was put upon
cabinet officials and upon politicians who were supposed to have influence with the new administration.[1]

The third volume of the *Writings of James Monroe*
contains twenty-two letters from that personage to
the new president. Fourteen of these have something to do with appointments. For instance,
among the applicants to be indorsed by Monroe
was Mr. Arthur Lee, of Norfolk. On September 25,
1801, Monroe wrote to Jefferson that Lee was a

[1] See, for example, Jefferson, *Writings* (Ford's ed.), VIII.,
26, 28, 34, 38, 40, 43, 46, 48, 51, 54, etc.

young man of merit, but three days later it occurred to him that he had been too complacent, and that Mr. Lee's object in going to Washington was to seek an office. Thereupon he sat down and wrote to Jefferson that he did not know what Mr. Lee's object might be, but that he was not well acquainted with that gentleman. He understood that Lee had delivered an interesting address on some recent occasion, but Monroe added that he was young, and he had heard him spoken of as "gay." If his object is the attainment of an office, the president should have much better information than his present correspondent could give.[1] That letter settled the case of Mr. Arthur Lee, of Norfolk.

One man in Washington was disgusted with it all —Albert Gallatin, the new secretary of the treasury. On July 25, thirteen days after Jefferson's New Haven letter, he presented to the president the draught of a circular which he wished to send to the collectors of customs. In this document the secretary proposed to call his subordinates' attention to the fact that the door of office is to be no longer shut against any man merely on account of his political opinions, as it had been under the Federalists. He added, however, that while freedom of opinion and freedom of suffrage are to be considered as imprescriptible rights, the president would regard any exercise of official influence to control the same rights in others as practically destructive of the fun-

[1] Monroe, *Writings*, III., 300, 301.

damental principles of a republican constitution.[1]
Jefferson said that he approved entirely of the two
paragraphs of which the circular was composed,
and stated that he had had some idea of issuing a
proclamation on the subject, but he and Madison
thought it would be better to wait until the New
Haven letter had produced its effect and until an
equilibrium had been established in the civil service.
After that had been accomplished, talents and
worth alone should be inquired into in the case of
new vacancies.   Neither the proclamation nor the
circular was ever issued.   Jefferson made less than
twenty removals for political reasons, mostly of
marshals and district attorneys.   The rest of the
removals of his time were for misconduct in office.
On March 4, 1801, there were 385 officials who were
subject to removal by the president.   Of these 183
were still in office March 4, 1805.   On the other
hand, when it fell to Jefferson's lot to appoint a full
set of commissioners of bankruptcy under the act
of 1801,[2] he distributed them impartially between
Republicans and Federalists.[3]

Ever since there has been any politics in America,
the twin storm-centres of political disturbance have
been New York and Pennsylvania, and so it was in
this case.   In New York, Aaron Burr and George

[1] Gallatin, *Writings* (Adams's ed.), I., 28.
[2] *Laws of the United States*, vi., 95; *U.S. Statutes at Large*, II., 164.
[3] As to removals, see Jefferson to Short, Jefferson, *Writings*
(Ford's ed.), IX., 51.

Clinton headed two rival factions. Burr's actions in the election of 1800 had filled Jefferson with disgust and loathing. When it came to distributing the spoils of office, he determined to use them to build up the Clinton faction, or, at all events, so as not to help Burr and his party workers. It was delicate business at best, and Burr was not at all disposed to aid the president in compassing his own downfall. Jefferson, with his usual finesse, let the brunt of the assault fall on Gallatin, for the secretary was on friendly terms with the vice-president. Burr made out his list of collector, naval officer, etc., of New York, but it would not go through.[1] The most important of these was Matthew L. Davis, Burr's right-hand man and afterwards his biographer. His appointment as naval officer in New York was urged by Burr and by Commodore Nicholson, Gallatin's father-in-law. The latter went so far as to inform his own son-in-law that if Burrites were not appointed to office in New York, when the next election came on he should work against Jefferson. This must have been distressing to the husband of Hannah Nicholson, but a month later the gallant commodore's political mouth was closed. He obtained a state office and became a Clintonian. As for Matthew L. Davis, he journeyed from New York to Monticello, Jefferson's residence. There he did not gain much satisfaction, for Jefferson said that nothing was decided; and

[1] See Jefferson, *Writings* (Ford's ed.), VIII., 52.

nothing ever was decided, as far as Davis was concerned, except that he, Burr's right-hand man, should not be appointed to office, although the carrying-out of this resolution required the retention in place of a man who had been a Tory in the Revolution. Six months later, we still find Burr writing to Gallatin on the subject, and imploring "the very small favor" of a decision as to Davis. The phrase "Nothing is determined" had become so commonplace to him that he would have preferred any other answer.

As to Pennsylvania, the case was perhaps more desperate; for William Duane, editor of the *Aurora*, was in the debtors' prison, with a host of doubtful friends clamoring for office. These were not exactly in the debtors' prison, but many of them were living not very remote from it. Duane appealed to Gallatin, and the secretary of the treasury resisted the sweeping removals urged by the *Aurora*. In this way began an enmity which in the end imbittered years of Gallatin's life.[1]

Of all of Jefferson's appointments and refusals to appoint, one shows a lack of political insight which, considering the man in error was Jefferson, is curious, to say the least. Among the men who have ever attained great distinction in American politics, no one would seem to come nearer to Jefferson than

[1] On the question of politics in New York and Pennsylvania, see Adams, *United States*, I., 228; Adams, *Gallatin*, 281; Gallatin, *Writings*, I., 34 et seq.

Andrew Jackson. Yet Andrew Jackson was one of the few ardent Republicans whom Jefferson absolutely refused to appoint to office. The issue arose in 1804, when the time was come to make arrangements for the government of a portion of the Louisiana purchase. The two senators from Tennessee and that state's four representatives united in recommending Jackson for the position of governor of Orleans territory. Jefferson, however, seems to have disliked the displays of temper which made Jackson popular with other classes in the community. He is said to have pronounced him a "dangerous man." This declaration was made many years later. We have no clew as to what were Jefferson's reasons for not appointing Jackson in 1804, except a letter written by William Henderson. In this letter Henderson says that he has been acquainted with Jackson for several years, and views him as a man of violent passion. At that moment, he declared, Jackson was being sued for assault and battery, and in a few days would surely be indicted for a breach of the peace. "Were it not for those despotic principles," wrote Henderson, "he might be a useful man."[1]

[1] There is an interesting article by Gaillard Hunt on "Office-seeking during Jefferson's Administration," in *Am. Hist. Rev.*, III., 270.

CHAPTER II

REPUBLICAN REFORMATIONS

(1801–1802)

IN the autumn of 1801, Jefferson, with his advisers, set to work to formulate a policy which should be enunciated in his first annual message to Congress. In Federalist times it had been customary for the president to make a speech at the opening of the session, to which the Houses separately responded in addresses. Anxious to do away with things monarchical, Jefferson had abandoned levees and now determined to send a written "message"[1] to which no formal answer would be expected; this mode of procedure possessed the further advantage that it saved Jefferson from the necessity of speaking in public, to which he was distinctly averse.

In the middle of November the president sent to Madison and to Gallatin the draught of the proposed document. He requested them to suggest such changes as seemed desirable. The message,[2] in its final form, is a remarkable document, both for what

[1] Jefferson, *Writings* (Ford's ed.), VIII., 108.
[2] Richardson, *Messages and Papers*, I., 326.

it contains and for what it does not contain. The
first thing that strikes one in its perusal is its studied
moderation in the matter of reform. Perhaps no
prophecy of Hamilton's rang more true than that
contained in his letter to Bayard of January 16,
1801,[1] in which he said that Jefferson would pursue
"a temporizing rather than a violent system."

One would have expected that the triumphant
author of the Kentucky Resolutions and his chief
adviser, who wrote the Virginia Resolutions, would
have attacked the very bases of the system which
had made those resolutions necessary. They did
nothing of the sort. The key to the conflict between
the nationalists like Hamilton and Marshall on the
one side, and the state-rights men like Jefferson and
Madison on the other, was in the supreme court of
the United States. At the moment that body was
composed entirely of Federalists whose appointments would continue for life. The new chief-
justice, John Marshall, of Virginia, presumably had
a long career before him, and his opinions on the
Constitution were perfectly well known to Jefferson.
The thing to do to carry out pre-election theories
was to get rid of John Marshall and the other judges
of the supreme court, or to neutralize their power.
The first could be done by the adoption of an amendment to the Constitution, changing the tenure of
the judges from life to four or six years; the second
could be accomplished by the appointment of enough

[1] Hamilton, *Works* (Lodge's ed.), VIII., 582.

judges to outvote Marshall and his Federalist companions, or by the alteration of the judiciary acts to impair seriously the activity of the supreme court. Jefferson advised none of these things. Instead of so doing, he merely suggested to Congress that the judiciary as organized under the act of 1801 was out of all proportion to the business it had to perform; there were, indeed, only eight cases on the docket of the supreme court. The same moderation is observable as to the army, the navy, and the financial system. As to the latter, indeed, he made some important suggestions. First, that effective steps should be taken towards paying the national debt, and, secondly, that "weighing all probabilities of expense, as well as of income, there is reasonable ground of confidence that we may now safely dispense with all the internal taxes."

At the time, and ever since, this great moderation of performance where so much was expected has been a fruitful source of comment. Yet the explanation seems to be not so very difficult. Jefferson received 73 electoral votes to 65 cast for John Adams. The election had been very close in South Carolina, where the presidential electors were appointed by the legislature, and the Republican electors had been chosen by a majority of from 15 to 18 votes in a total of 151. The change of nine votes in that legislature would have given the electoral vote of South Carolina and the election itself to the Federalists. The revolution of 1800 had been won by a very narrow margin. Moreover, when the new Congress met, and a controversial subject came up, it was found that in the Senate 15 votes were given for the administration and 15 were given against it. At the moment when this vote was taken, two Republican senators were absent, so that we might place the normal Republican majority in the Senate at two. In the House the case was decidedly better for the Republicans, as the bill to repeal the Judiciary Act passed the lower House by a majorty of 59 to 32. The ability and power in debate, however, was so clearly with the 32 that, at one time, the majority refused to talk at all, and simply voted down any motion made by the minority. It earned in this way the title of "the dumb legislature," but it did not expose its weak debaters to the hazard of being overpowered.

If the administration was weak in Congress, its weakness was much greater even in the strong Democratic states of the north. In New York and Pennsylvania the Republicans held a large majority, but in both of those states the Republican politicians, having no effective opponents in the Federalist party, had taken to fighting among themselves. It was problematical, to say the least, how long Jefferson and his administration would retain the allegiance of any or of all the warring factions. It behooved the party managers, therefore, to look elsewhere in the north for that assistance without which the solid south has never been able to control the government. This new support must be found in New England, for at that time there was no "middle west" which had voting representatives in Congress. To the conversion of New England, therefore, Jefferson must look for his political salvation; and nothing would have made the political conversion of New England more difficult than the forcing through of radical reforms. Besides, it is no doubt true that Jefferson, like other rulers, whether great or small, saw things with a different eye when he himself administered the government and when he was in opposition.

The Federalist legislation of recent years which had most angered the Republican opposition were the Alien and Sedition acts, the Naturalization Act, and the Judiciary Act. Of these, the Alien and Sedition acts had expired by limitation. The new Congress repealed the Naturalization Act, substituting in its place the law of 1795, which required a five years' period of residence for citizenship in place of the fourteen demanded by the law of 1798.[1] With regard to the Judiciary Act, the question of its repeal raised several interesting points. The act of 1801 had provided for the organization of a new set of federal courts midway between the supreme court and the district courts, with judges, attorneys, and marshals of their own.[2] At one time Jefferson

---

[1] *Laws of the United States*, VI., 74 (Acts of 1 Sess. of 7 Cong., chap. xxviii.); *U. S. Statutes at Large*, II., 53.

[2] See Bassett, *Federalist System*, chap. xvii.

himself seems to have felt that under the Constitution all federal judges, when they had once been commissioned, held a species of freehold in their office, and could not be displaced except by impeachment. This view was naturally enforced with a wealth of argument and denunciation which the skilled debaters on the Federalist side were amply able to pour forth. The quality of political debates of that time may be judged from the following extract from the speech of Representative Bayard, one of the leading Federalist speakers: "There are many now willing to spill their blood to defend that constitution. . . . If gentlemen are regardless of themselves, let them consider their wives and children, their neighbors and their friends. Will they risk civil dissention; will they hazard the welfare, will they jeopardize the peace of the country to save a paltry sum of money, less than 30,000 dollars?" To this the Republicans answered that these new circuit courts existed solely by virtue of an act of Congress, and could be destroyed by Congress whenever it saw fit. The question at issue was not the displacement of the judges, or the saving of thirty or forty thousand dollars, although, of course, economy in the national expenditures was one of the points which the Republicans had most at heart in their general scheme of reform. As to the judges, although the sanctity of the office was admitted, it was felt that Adams had acted with extreme partisanship in filling all those posi-

tions with Federalists in the last sixteen days of
his administration; the judiciary had become "a
hospital for decayed politicians."[1] What especially
angered the Republicans in the new judiciary system was the fact that under it recourse to the federal
courts would be more easy. The federal jurisdiction
would be extended at the expense of the state courts.
The repeal was carried, however, by one vote in
the Senate[2] and only after a most acrimonious discussion in the House. In the Senate, at one time,
on the question of referring the repealing bill to a
select committee, the vote stood even, and Vice-
President Burr, by the use of his casting-vote,
secured the reference to the committee and showed
his hostility to the administration.[3] In fact, so peculiar was Burr's position that he was invited by
the Federalists to a banquet. Entering the room,
he assumed the seat of honor and soon proposed a
toast to the "union of all honest men." From the
context, so to speak, there could be little doubt that
Burr did not include the president among those to
whom the toast was drunk.

In repealing the Judiciary Act the Republicans
also recurred to the old arrangements. They reduced the terms of the supreme court to one an-
nually, which should commence on the first Monday
of February, and which might be held by any four

[1] John Randolph, of Roanoke, used this contemptuous expression.   [2] *Annals of Cong.*, 7 Cong., 1 Sess., 183.
[3] *Ibid.*, 150.

of the judges. One advantage of this arrangement at that particular moment was that the law repealing the Judiciary Act of 1801 would go into effect at once, before Marshall and his associates on the supreme bench could declare it unconstitutional, as the next session of the supreme court would not be held until February, 1803. In the future, six courts were established, in each of which a single justice of the supreme court, with a district judge, should decide all cases brought before them. In cases where they differed on points of law, the matter should be certified to the supreme court for decision. With some modifications in detail this system continued in force for more than half a century.[1]

The most important event of the session was the establishment of a new financial policy. Jefferson argued very strongly for economy, and Gallatin outdid his chief in this respect.[2] In his comments on the draught of Jefferson's first message, Gallatin insisted strongly on three things. These were, first, the payment of seven millions each year on the interest and principal of the national debt; second, on every possible reduction of taxation which could be made; third, on Congress making specific appropriations, and on a simplification of the organization and workings of the treasury and the spend-

---

[1] See *Laws of the United States*, VI., 15, 83 (Acts of 1 Sess. of 7 Cong., chaps. viii., xxxi.); *U. S. Statutes at Large*, II., 132, 156.
[2] Jefferson, *Writings* (Ford's ed.), VIII., 109.

ing departments. It will be well to examine these
three points somewhat in detail.

First as to the national debt. Hamilton, in his
report of 1789, had estimated the national debt,
including arrears of interest and state debts to be
assumed, at $76,000,000 in round numbers. On
January 1, 1802, the debt stood at over $80,000,000,
and on January 1, 1803, the net debt was given by
Gallatin as $77,000,000. That year saw the pay-
ment of $15,000,000 for Louisiana, which was made
by means of a loan. In the same year, however,
over five and a half millions were paid on account of
the principal of the debt. From that time until
1810, there was a steady decrease in the amount of
the national debt, until in 1810 it stood at a little
over $53,000,000, the decrease in eight years be-
ing almost exactly $27,500,000, in the face of the
$15,000,000 paid for Louisiana and the money doled
out most ungraciously by Gallatin on the navy. In
November, 1801, Gallatin estimated the revenue
for the next year at $10,600,000. Of this he pro-
posed to use $3,600,000 in payment of the interest,
and of more than $3,500,000 to pay the current
expenses of the government, including the army
and the navy. These figures are the best justification of Gallatin's remarkable financial achievement.
For it cannot be denied that, when the interest on
the national debt required nearly one-third of the
revenue, it was time to take effective measures to
relieve the country of so great a burden.

The only possible way to accomplish this result, which Gallatin so much desired, was to pursue a steady and prolonged career of economy; and to do that it was absolutely necessary that the country should remain at peace with all the nations. Gallatin seems to have had no such rooted dislike to a naval establishment as was entertained by Jefferson. His dislike of a navy at the then juncture of affairs was due to the fact that he thought a navy was likely to bring trouble to the country which would cost money. Until the debt was paid, he was disposed to follow the old precept of turning the other cheek to the smiter. When the debt is paid then will be the time to build ships—and not before.

In his comment on Jefferson's message, Gallatin wrote in a very guarded manner as to the repeal of the internal taxes: he would like to do it, if he could see a surplus without those revenues. The only way to bring this about, however, was by securing reforms in the army and the navy departments which should lead to a better accountability in those departments, and to the United States getting a better return for its money. Jefferson was more courageous than his secretary, and mentioned the repeal of the internal taxes as being within the bounds of reason.[1]

When the new Congress assembled, Nathaniel Macon was chosen speaker of the House. He was an admirable example of the plantation type of

[1] Richardson, Messages and Papers, I., 328.

statesman which was now to dominate national life. Buck Spring, his North Carolina plantation, had for him the same absorbing charm that Monticello had for Jefferson. Unlike the latter, however, he did not note the unearthing of the bones of megatheriums; but he atoned for his neglect by recording the births of his thorough-breds on a fly-leaf of the family Bible.[1] He had been long in public life, was familiar with the rules of parliamentary procedure, was of a judicial cast of mind, and was admirably fitted for his new post. An intimate friend of John Randolph, of Roanoke, and admiring his courage and capacity, he appointed him chairman of the committee of ways and means. As long as Jefferson, Randolph, and Macon acted in harmony, affairs were likely to go in the way true Republicans wished.

The committee on ways and means had been first appointed in 1796, on motion of Gallatin, when the Republicans were in control of the House but not of the executive department, in order to wrench from the Federalist secretary of the treasury a portion of the control of the national finances. John Randolph, who now became chairman of this most important committee, was one of the most remarkable figures in that wonderful galaxy of Virginians of the past. Belonging to the greatest family of the Old Dominion, he was heavily in debt, and absolutely without experience in the manage-

[1] Dodd, *Nathaniel Macon*, 371.

ment of financial affairs—except so far as he had
tried to unravel his brother's and his own—and
without any success whatever. This was the man
who now became the financial mouthpiece of Jefferson and Gallatin. It must be confessed that in this
capacity he exhibited vastly greater financial ability
than he showed in the management of his own es-
tates. Sending for the secretaries of war and of
the navy, he secured from them pledges of economy [1]
which made Gallatin give his consent to the repeal of all internal taxes. The result showed that
Gallatin was right in his lack of faith in naval economy. It also showed that Randolph was right in
his faith in the redundancy of the national revenues. For Gallatin, with characteristic caution,
had underestimated his receipts, while giving his expenditures at very nearly their correct figure. In
this way went the internal revenue system, and
with it about one-quarter of the patronage of the
federal government—a sacrifice of political power
to which few other men than Thomas Jefferson
would have consented. [2]

As to the third point noted above. Gallatin
deliberately asked Congress to curtail his own
power by making appropriations for specific purposes. He also secured the simplification of the

---

[1] Details are given in the reports of the ways and means
committee in *History of the Last Session of Congress*, 1802, p. 182.

[2] The repealing act is printed in *Laws of the United States*,
VI., 58 (Acts of 1 Sess., 7 Cong., chap. xix.); *U. S. Statutes at
Large*, II., 148.

service to bring about greater direct responsibility
to himself as the head of the treasury department.
The system established by Gallatin remains to this
day, and is undoubtedly one of the most perfect or-
ganizations of a great financial machine which can
be found anywhere in the world.

In 1802 that portion of the territory northwest
of the Ohio which was included within the limits of
the present state of that name was admitted to the
Union as the state of Ohio.[1] William B. Giles,
another Virginia politician, was appointed chairman of the committee of the House of Representatives which had charge of this matter. February
13, 1802, Gallatin[2] wrote to Giles suggesting that, in
admitting the new state to the Union, Congress
might make an arrangement which would be advantageous to Ohio and to the United States. This
was to secure to the national government the same
rights as to the national domain within the state that
it had had during the territorial period. As the
state legislature could hardly be expected to give
this boon to the United States without compensation, Gallatin suggested that section No. 16 in
every township sold should be granted to the inhabitants of such townships for the use of schools;
and, furthermore, that one-tenth part of the net
proceeds of the lands within the limits of the state,

---

[1] *Laws of the United States*. VI., 120 (chap. xl.); *U. S. Statutes
at Large*, II., 173.
[2] Gallatin, *Writings* (Adams's ed.), I., 76.

hereafter sold by Congress, should be applied towards making roads to the Ohio River from the navigable waters emptying into the Atlantic, and afterwards to roads within the state—such roads to be laid out under the authority of Congress. The provisions for schools had been included in a former ordinance of Congress. As to the building of roads, Gallatin thought that such a system of communication would be beneficial to the northwest territory itself, and from a political point of view would contribute "towards cementing the bonds of the Union between those parts of the United States whose local interests have been considered as most dissimilar." Congress was not so liberal as Gallatin, and offered only five per cent. for roads and one-thirty-sixth part of the land for the schools. Ohio accepted the proposition. In this way began the splendid provision for education which marks the states erected on the national domain, and Jefferson, Gallatin, and John Randolph laid the foundation for the first great internal improvement. It was an extraordinary performance when one considers that it emanated from the apostles of "strict construction"; but statesmen out of power and in office oftentimes do acts which no amount of argument can make to appear consistent.

The revolution of 1800, besides placing the government in the hands of the Republicans as a political organization, had operated to give supreme power in national affairs to southern slave-holders;

but when these sought to protect their interests as owners of negroes, northern Democrats refused to follow them. This was shown by the action of the House on a fugitive-slave bill which was brought in on December 18, 1801. In this measure it was proposed to impose a fine of five hundred dollars on any one anywhere in the United States who should employ a strange negro without first advertising a description of the man in two newspapers, as was the practice in some southern states. The Republican members from the north, with only half a dozen exceptions, voted against it. The bill was lost by a vote of 46 to 43, although several southern Federalists joined the Jeffersonians. This attempt on the part of the Republican slaveholding leaders to use their power to protect their "property" marked the limit to which northern subserviency was willing to go; in other respects, however, the Jeffersonian reformations were generally acceptable to the rank and file of the party. This fidelity to party is especially noticeable in the debates on reapportionment, in which the effect of a proposed ratio is considered more in reference to party than to state affiliations.[1]

[1] See debates as printed in *History of the Last Session of Congress*, 1802, pp. 45, 46.

CHAPTER III

THE TRIPOLITAN WAR

(1801–1804)

OF all the Federalist inventions nothing was more hateful to Jefferson than the navy. April 17, 1801, he wrote to Samuel Smith that he should be chagrined if he could not lay up the seven larger. men-of-war in the eastern branch of the Potomac, where the ships would be under the immediate eye of the department, and would require but "one set of plunderers to take care of them." [1] The difficulty oppressed him day and night. This sentence occurs in a letter offering the secretaryship of the navy to the Maryland congressman Samuel Smith. He was not willing to undertake so discouraging a task, especially because it would require him to abandon his business pursuits. For some months, however, he administered the affairs of the department without an appointment and without compensation— in that way avoiding the resignation of his seat in the House of Representatives. Eventually, the position was given to his brother, Robert Smith. Jefferson was never able wholly to carry out his plan,

[1] Adams, *United States*, I., 223.

but by December five of the seven frigates were laid up at the Washington navy-yard, where they were kept in such condition as to be at all times ready for sea on a short warning. In his second annual message to Congress (December 15, 1802), he suggested that a new dock should be built at the Washington navy-yard within which the vessels might be "laid up dry and under cover from the sun"[1]— which reminds one of Queen Elizabeth's objections to sending the vessels of the royal navy to sea lest their paint might be injured. Jefferson and Gallatin were certainly most desirous to limit naval expenditure in every possible way; but they reckoned without the North African pirates. Indeed, instead of laying up the ships high and dry on the shore, they were obliged to send fleet after fleet to the Mediterranean and to build new vessels better suited for work in those waters.

Few things are more astonishing in the international history of the eighteenth century than the payment of tribute to the Barbary powers by the great maritime nations of Europe. In the case of England, this seems to have been done as a matter of policy; for in this way she was able to monopolize a large part of the trade between the Mediterranean and the seaports of the Atlantic.

When the United States won its independence, its commerce was no longer protected by the British tribute, and within two years of the signing of the

[1] Richardson, *Messages and Papers*, I., 345.

treaty of peace an Algerine corsair captured two American vessels.[1] In 1793, after a period of quietude, the Algerines suddenly seized eleven American merchant-men with one hundred and twelve seamen and passengers, who were enslaved. Trouble, also, was threatening with England, and this, with the activity of the pirates, led to the building of the first ships of the American navy since the close of the Revolutionary War. These vessels were the forty-four-gun frigates *Constitution, President,* and *United States,* and the thirty-six-gun frigates *Chesapeake, Congress,* and *Constellation.* These vessels embodied in their construction the very best ideas of naval architecture of that day. They proved to be the finest ships of their class then in existence. While they were in process of construction, more than a million dollars in presents and money were paid to the dey of Algiers, in addition to an annual tribute of $22,000. This payment quieted him for only a few months, and another million had to be paid in 1796. Hardly was this money expended when approaching troubles with France induced Congress to vote nearly a million dollars for the building of a fleet of small naval vessels. During the war with France which followed, besides the vessels of the regular navy, the government used

[1] The events touched upon in this chapter are admirably set forth by Gardner W. Allen, *Our Navy and the Barbary Corsairs* (1905). A shorter account is in Soley's chapter on "Wars of the United States," in Winsor, *America* (VII., 359-375, and bibliography, 417-420).

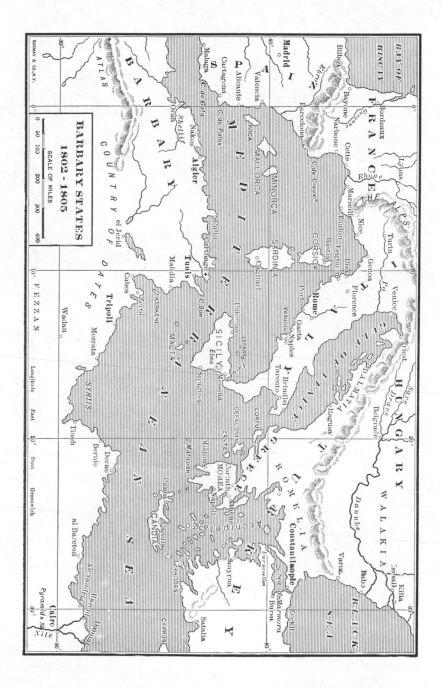

revenue-cutters and a number of converted merchant-men. In 1800 the prospect of peace induced
Congress to order the reduction of the naval force
to fifteen vessels, and this reduction was already
proceeding when Jefferson became president.

Yusuf Caramelli, pacha of Tripoli, received an
annual tribute from the United States government
of $83,000 in money and presents. He felt aggrieved,
and insisted that the rulers of Algiers, Tunis, and
Morocco received more money than he—considering their relative importance. May 14, 1801, he cut
down the flag-staff at the American consulate in
Tripoli, which was the Barbary method of declaring
war. A year before this the dey of Algiers had
pressed the American war-ship *George Washington*
into service to carry presents and envoys to Constantinople.[1] He even compelled Captain Bainbridge to hoist the Algerine flag at his mast. As
soon as the *George Washington* was clear of the harbor, Bainbridge hauled down the Mohammedan en-
sign and replaced it with "Old Glory," which, at
the time, had fifteen stripes and fifteen stars. When
the war-ship anchored off Constantinople, the sul-
tan was much pleased with the star-spangled ban-
ner, in which he seemed to find something kindred
to his own crescent. In the early summer of 1801
the *George Washington* reached the United States
with the story of the outrages which had been per-
petrated on her and on the American flag.

[1] Harris, *Bainbridge*, 44; Allen, *Barbary Corsairs*, 75–87.

Jefferson had not waited for the news of any fresh exactions, but on May 20, .six days after the flag-staff cutting at Tripoli, but long before the report reached him, he had ordered Commodore Dale to the Mediterranean with the *President*, *Philadelphia*, and the schooner *Enterprise*. This squadron was soon reinforced by the thirty-two-gun frigate *Essex*, with which Captain Bainbridge returned to the scene of his recent humiliation.

Commodore Dale, on arriving at Gibraltar, found two Tripolitan corsairs there, lying in wait for American merchant-men. Leaving the *Philadelphia* to watch them, with the other two vessels he sailed for Algiers. On August 1 the *Enterprise*, being then alone on detached duty, captured a Tripolitan cruiser of fourteen guns. President Jefferson, with a proper regard for the strict construction of the Constitution,[1] which gives to Congress the right of declaring war, had instructed Commodore Dale that in the event of his taking a Barbary corsair he should dismantle the ship, throw her guns and gunpowder into the sea, and let her go with just enough sail to reach port. Lieutenant Sterrett, the commander of the *Enterprise*, carried out these directions,[2] and with most fortunate results, for the crew of the *Tripoli*, when they reached their home port, gave such heartrending accounts of the ferocious

[1] Jefferson, *Writings* (Ford's ed.), I., 293, gives minutes of a cabinet meeting on this subject.
[2] *Am. State Paps.*, *Naval*, I., 82.

qualities of the sailors from beyond the Atlantic that the pacha of Tripoli found it difficult to bring his men up to the fighting-line again. Meantime the *President* visited the dey of Algiers and the pacha of Tripoli, and showed to those potentates the kind of American ship which was likely to visit them if they did not mend their ways.

The year 1802 saw Commodore Richard Valentine Morris in the Mediterranean, with four frigates, two corvettes, and the *Enterprise*. But this large force accomplished little besides worrying the Barbary pirates, and Commodore Morris on his return to the United States was dismissed from the service.

The next year (1803) the war was conducted with greater vigor. Captain Edward Preble was now in command of the fleet. The first exploit was the capture by the *Philadelphia* of the Moorish ship *Meshboha*, or *Mirboka*, belonging to the emperor of Morocco. As there was some doubt as to the authority under which the captain of this vessel had seized an American brig, Commodore Preble visited Tangiers with the *Constitution*, the *New York*, the *John Adams*, and the *Nautilus*. The emperor at once disavowed the act of his captain, fired twenty-one guns as a salute to the American flag, and promised to behave better in the future.

Soon after this, while the *Philadelphia* was chasing a Tripolitan vessel in the vicinity of the mouth of that harbor, she ran hard and fast on a reef. Her guns were thrown overboard, water was pumped out, and the foremast was cut away. Nothing was of any avail; the ship was soon surrounded by a fleet of Tripolitan gun-boats, which could take any position they chose and attack without fear of damage to themselves. Under these circumstances Captain Bainbridge surrendered.[1] Not long afterwards a heavy gale from the north piled up the water on the African coast. The *Philadelphia* was floated, her guns were raised, and she was anchored in the harbor of Tripoli as an additional defence to the pacha's castle. The idea of destroying her as she lay at anchor seems to have occurred to several persons at about the same time. It is impossible to say whether the credit for the inception of the enterprise should be given to Commodore Preble, Captain Bainbridge, or Lieutenant Stephen Decatur. There is not the slightest doubt, however, that the destruction of the ship was owing to the gallant manner in which Decatur executed Preble's orders. The story is one which is familiar to every American school-boy, but it can never be told too often

In a little Mediterranean vessel called the *Mastico* when she was captured, but rechristened the *Intrepid*, as descriptive of her new mission, Decatur, with seventy-five men, sailed boldly into the harbor of Tripoli, which was defended by twenty-five thousand men and one hundred and fifty guns, more or less. Ranging alongside the *Philadelphia*, a sudden cast of wind caused the *Intrepid* to shear

[1] Bainbridge's report is in *Am. State Paps.*, *Naval*, I., 123.

away from the frigate's side. With a calmness
given only to heroes, Decatur got out a boat
while the Tripolitans were looking on, made fast
a line to the frigate's cable, and slowly warped
the little boat right under the war-ship's broadside. As he had almost reached his chosen place,
a Tripolitan spied the seamen lying prone on
the *Intrepid's* deck and shouted, "Americanos!
Americanos!" Instantly all was uproar on the
frigate, but, scrambling on board over the bulwarks
and through the open ports, the assailants charged
the enemy. The Tripolitans stood not on the order
of their going; without waiting the onslaught, they
leaped into the harbor, where many of them were
killed by the crew of the boat which had carried the
line to the *Philadelphia's* cable. Decatur thought
that at least twenty Tripolitans were killed on the
ship. Combustibles, with which the *Intrepid* was
laden, were then passed over the side. Within
twenty-five minutes from the time he first gained
her deck, Decatur, with his gallant crew, were back
on his boat again, and the *Philadelphia* was a mass
of flames. Amid a storm of shot from the forts
and the gun-boats and from the guns of the *Philadelphia* herself, Decatur and his heroic comrades[1]
swept out of the harbor and gained the open
sea.

In the winter of 1803–1804, Preble's squadron

---

[1] The roster of the *Intrepid's* officers and crew is in *Am. State
Paps., Naval*, I., 128.

was reinforced by three or four smaller vessels which
had been built for service in the shallow waters of
northern Africa. Jefferson, Madison, and Gallatin
disliked and dreaded a strong navy for many and
quite different reasons. They recognized, however,
that the Tripolitan War would better be vigorously
prosecuted or not waged at all. As they determined
to pay no more tribute, the only alternative was
war. Jefferson found in Robert Smith a secretary
of the navy who enjoyed the backing of a strong
political faction at home and personal popularity
in the service. Before the Federalists left office
they had provided for the reduction of the navy by
the sale of the least efficient vessels. Of the smaller
vessels whose retention or sale was within the discretion of the president, he kept one only—the
Enterprise. The new ships which were built in
1803 embodied in their construction all the most
valuable features which the experience of the English, the French, and our own sailors had taught.
They were at the moment the best vessels of their
class afloat. Their names were *Siren*, *Argus*, *Nautilus*, and *Vixen*. With his fleet augmented by
gun-boats and bomb-ketches which had been bor-
rowed from the king of Sicily, who happened to be
at war with the pacha of Tripoli, Commodore Preble
bombarded Tripoli once and again.[1] In these at-
tacks the Americans showed great gallantry, and

[1] This part of the Tripolitan Wars is well set forth in Sabine,
Life of Edward Preble.

they undoubtedly served to make the pacha more
amenable to reason.

In the course of this warfare an event happened
which resulted in the death of Richard Somers
and a half-dozen gallant companions. It occurred
to Preble, or to one of his subordinates, that if the
Intrepid, laden with explosives, were taken into the
midst of the Tripolitan gun-boats and there ex-
ploded, some of those boats would surely be destroyed, and the nerves of the pacha would be still
more shaken. On a dark night, therefore, Somers
sailed into the harbor. Before he fairly entered
he was attacked by several gun-boats, whose crews
swarmed on board the fire-ship. At that moment,
Somers, it is supposed, jumped into the hold with a
lighted lantern and blew himself, his comrades,
and his enemies into the air.[1]

The final event which brought the Tripolitan
pacha to a realizing sense of the necessity of making
peace was the appearance of his elder brother with
a motley force on the frontiers of his kingdom.
His name was Hamet Caramelli, and he had been
driven into exile by the usurping Yusuf, the reigning
pacha. His coming at this time was due mainly to the fantastic ideas of a Connecticut Yankee named William Eaton. Without any direct authorization from the American government, Eaton
and Hamet raised an army of some five hundred
men and set out from Alexandria, in Egypt, to march

[1] Allen, *Barbary Corsairs*, 207.

five hundred miles, much of it across a desert. Instead of succumbing to hunger or thirst or mutiny, in place of being killed by wandering Arabs, Eaton and Hamet captured the Tripolitan town of Derne and overran the eastern half of Yusuf's or Hamet's kingdom.[1] Now, at length, Pacha Yusuf listened to reason. He agreed to live in the future at peace with America without any tribute and to hand over the officers and crew of the *Philadelphia* on payment of $60,000. For ten years the Barbary rulers treated the Americans with respect. Then, after the War of 1812 was over, Commodore Decatur, as he then was, with a squadron revisited the waters of his earlier career and negotiated a fresh set of treaties literally at the cannon's mouth. As for Hamet, he was transported to a place of safety and given a pension of $200 per month, and his followers were left to the resentment of Yusuf.

[1] On this episode, see Eaton's side of the case in Prentiss, *Life of General William Eaton*.

CHAPTER IV

LA LOUISIANE

(1684–1800)

DREAMS of colonial empire have always powerfully agitated the French imagination. Not that Frenchmen themselves have ever wished to become colonists; they have always hoped that other Frenchmen would go and settle in far-off regions and build up an empire beyond the seas. Of all their colonies, none has a more interesting history to Americans than Louisiana.

To La Salle, the greatest of Franco-American explorers, was due the first idea of a French colony on the Mississippi River. But his expedition, in 1684, missed its destination and landed on the coast of Texas, and he himself met an untimely end while on a search for the great river.[1] In 1699 a new

---

[1] Cf. Thwaites, *France in America* (*Am. Nation*, VII.), chap. iv. The late Dr. Gilmary Shea maintained that La Salle's real object was the conquest of a portion of Mexico, and that he went intentionally to Texas. See Ficklen, *Louisiana Purchase*, 5, *n*. (Southern History Association, *Publications*).

and more fortunate French expedition sailed into the Gulf of Mexico. Pensacola was found to be occupied by the Spaniards. Proceeding onward, therefore, the first settlement of the modern Louisiana was made either on the shores of Mobile Bay or at some point in its vicinity.[1] A little stream, the Rio de los Perdidos, the river of the lost, or the Perdido River, to give it its English name, was recognized as the boundary between the Spanish and French settlements. Iberville, the sea-commander of this expedition, returned almost at once to France. After his departure, Bienville, the shore-commander, explored the Mobile River and the lower Mississippi. On this latter expedition he came across an English ship which turned and sailed out of the river, and this encounter led to the establishment of a fort on Poverty Point, which was the first French post on the great river. New Orleans itself seems to have been founded in 1718; it became the principal town of the colony in 1720.[2]

The two most attractive features in the life of the northern French colony of New France were the amicable relations which were established with the Indians and the development on the soil of the New World of a modified form of French feudalism. Neither of these is found reproduced in the southern

[1] Hamilton, *Colonial Mobile*, chap. vi.
[2] On the foundation of Louisiana, see Thwaites, *France in America* (*Am. Nation*, VII.), chap. v.

colony of Louisiana. The precise reason for this difference is not clear. Possibly the fact that the Jesuits never obtained a spiritual monopoly on the banks of the Mississippi may have had something to do with the failure as to the Indians. Land in Louisiana was always held directly of the government, under certain reasonable conditions as to its improvement, and seigneurs with their body-guard of banalités and censitaires were not there reproduced. Louisiana grew with painful slowness. Ever-recurring starvation and Indian hostility more than once threatened the life of the settlement. In time, however, Indian traders penetrated to the interior west of the Mississippi. In 1723 the culture of indigo was introduced; but Louisiana indigo never had a good reputation and in time ceased to be a staple. The cultivation of sugar was begun by the Jesuit fathers in 1751. The sugar grown in the next few years was used in the making of spirits. In 1765 a cargo of sugar was exported from the colony; but it was so poorly crystallized that it leaked out of the hogsheads on the voyage to France, and the venture proved to be disastrous. From that time on until near the close of the century sugar was cultivated only for purposes of distillation. In 1794 an enterprising planter named Boré began again the cultivation of sugar amid the jeers of his neighbors. He sold his first crop for $12,000. In 1795 the cultivation of cotton was introduced, and the future of Louisiana was assured. In 1802 the exports of the province were as follows:[1]

20,000	bales of cotton..............	$1,344,000	increasing
45,000	casks of sugar...............	302,400	"
800	casks of molasses............	32,000	"
	Indigo......................	100,000	decreasing
	Peltry......................	200,000	"
	Lumber.....................	80,000	"
	Lead, corn, horses, cattle....	uncertain	"
	All other articles, supposed....	100,000	"
		$2,158,400	

In addition to these articles, government vessels carried away large quantities of naval stores. This commerce was transacted in American and Spanish vessels, the American vessels outnumbering the Spanish ships nearly two to one—not counting public ships.

The cultivation of sugar and cotton in the rich bottom-lands of the lower Mississippi was fatal to white immigrants to Louisiana, as the cultivation of rice under similar conditions was fatal to new settlers in South Carolina. It followed from this that negro slavery was inevitable in Louisiana as it was in the English colony. In both cases the laws prescribing the treatment of slaves were drawn from the existing codes of the West India Islands. Thus it fell out that South Carolina reproduced the laws of the English Barbadoes, and Louisiana had a combination of French and Spanish colonial slave regulations. Slaves were held in large numbers on the Louisiana plantations, and they were of recent

[1] *Am. State Paps., Misc.*, I., 354.

importation for the most part. In 1803, therefore, the addition of Louisiana to the United States meant the addition of a new centre of negro slavery of the extremest type.

Until 1763 Louisiana lived a life of its own, removed from the influence of the outer world, except so far as it was French. In 1763, however, Louisiana was handed over by France to Spain to make good the loss which the latter had sustained in coming to her aid in the tremendous contest with the Anglo-Saxon. After a delay of some years, and then with a good deal of difficulty, the Spaniards took possession of their new colony, and it remained Spanish until its acquisition by the United States. A generation of Spanish rule powerfully affected the laws and institutions of the colony.

The legal institutions of France and Spain were both founded on the civil law, but the official government of Louisiana in the Spanish régime was that of a Spanish colony under the new laws of the Indies.[1] Under these laws there were only eight capital crimes, but offences not capital were punished with the mines of Mexico or the dungeons of Morro Castle and Cabañas at Havana.

The government of Louisiana was mainly in the hands of three officers—the governor, the contador,

[1] See Don John O'Reilly's "Regulations" in the *Recopilacion de Leyes de las Indias* and *Novissima Recopilacion de las Leyes de España*. Most of these may be found in English in the *Am. State Paps, Public Lands*, V., and *Misc.*, I.; they are substantially given in White, *New Recopilacion*.

and the intendant. The latter name and office came down from the French period, but was preserved throughout the time of Spanish control. The governor was the civil and military head of the colony, the intendant had control of the revenue and commerce, and the contador, or treasurer, was little more than a financial clerk. The door of the treasure-house had three locks, the keys of which were held by these three officials, whose united presence was necessary for access to the treasure-chests. It is necessary to note carefully that under this system the intendant was entirely out of the control of the governor and was frequently opposed to him.

In the French time there had been a council which represented pretty faithfully the desires of the colonists. For this the Spaniards substituted a cabildo, which was a species of appointed town council whose members obtained their places by purchase. The cabildo, besides its local functions, acted as an advisory board for the government, had to do with the appointment of the lesser judges, and also exercised some police power.[1] It was, in short, a municipal council, superior court, police commission, board of health, and advisory council for the governor all in one. When Louisiana was retroceded to France, Napoleon intended to introduce a somewhat different form of government.

---

[1] See "An Account of Louisiana," in *Am. State Paps.*, *Misc.*, I.; and Thwaites, *France in America* (*Am. Nation*, VII.), chap. xviii.

But the later French occupation, if so it can be named, was too short to do more than to introduce new complications into an already involved system.

In 1763 Louisiana was ceded by the king of France to his cousin, the king of Spain, so far as it included the territory west of the Mississippi River and the island on which New Orleans stands. This island extends along the eastern side of the river for the last 229 miles of its course. The Spaniards, therefore, controlled the navigation of the Mississippi. At the same time that the king of France handed over this vast region to Spain he acknowledged the king of Great Britain to be the rightful possessor of all of Louisiana east of the Mississippi, with the exception of the island of Orleans. This cession included the port of Mobile. As a part of the same great international settlement, Spain handed over to Great Britain her claim to the soil of the continent of North America east of Louisiana, or, in other words, Florida, with boundaries according to the Spanish pretensions. In the French treaty, the king of France guaranteed to the king of Great Britain the freedom of the Mississippi "from its source to the sea, and expressly that part which is between the said Island of Orleans and the right bank of that river, as well as the passage both in and out of its mouth." It will be seen from this statement that Great Britain acquired, in 1763, a clear title to Florida and to all of Louisiana east

of the Mississippi and east of the island of Orleans.[1]

The English king made a curious disposal of this
region.[2] In the first place he established the government of East Florida with the limits included in
the present state of Florida east of the Appalachi-
cola River. Spanish Florida west of this river and
Louisiana east of lakes Maurepas and Pontchar-
train and south of the thirty-first parallel of north
latitude he formed into the government of West
Florida. It will be well for the reader to bear carefully in mind the way in which this little piece of
Louisiana between the lakes and the Perdido River
was treated in 1763, inasmuch as that bit of territory,
in later time, became the subject of active controversy.

Not content with thus laying trouble for future
generations, the English government soon extended
the limits of West Florida to embrace within the
jurisdiction of the governor of that province the
French settlement of Natchez, on the east bank of
the Mississippi. This enlargement was effected,
not by making a new proclamation, but by extending the bounds of the governor's authority in the
successive commissions which were issued.[3] This

[1] See the "King's Proclamation of 1763," in the *Annual
Register* for that year, 208–213, or *Am. Hist. Leaflets*, No. 5.
[2] See also Thwaites, *France in America* (*Am. Nation*, VII.),
chap. xvii.
[3] See Duane, *Laws of the United States*, I., 452, or *Am. Hist.
Leaflets*, No. 5.

arrangement, which has so puzzled politicians and students of the nineteenth century, may well have puzzled Spanish governors and ministers of the eighteenth century. Such was the condition of affairs when Spain intervened in the conflict between the American colonists and Great Britain.

When the negotiators signed the preliminary articles of peace at Paris in 1782,[1] they combined to make a curious arrangement which has added to the perplexities of students of American history. In the treaty they provided that the southern boundary of the United States between the Mississippi and the Chattahoochee rivers should be the thirty-first parallel. In a separate article it was provided that in case Great Britain, at the conclusion of the war then raging, should be in possession of West Florida, the southern boundary of the United States should be the parallel of the confluence of the Yazoo and the Mississippi rivers, or, approximately, the latitude 32° 30′. As it turned out, the British were unable to drive the Spaniards out of West Florida. The definite treaty of peace between the United States and Great Britain which was signed in 1783 defines, therefore, the southern boundary of the United States as the thirty-first parallel from the Mississippi to the Chattahoochee River. At the same time the British king ceded to Spain the Floridas without mentioning any boun-

[1] *Treaties and Conventions between the United States and Other Powers* (ed. of 1873), 312.

daries whatever. Here were the seeds of a neat little debate, and it was not long before the disputation began.[1]

After the Revolutionary War brave and resolute settlers passed the Alleghanies, cleared farms in the northwest territory, in Kentucky, and in the region south of Kentucky. These pioneers were among the most ardent disciples of democracy anywhere to be found. The only outlet for their lumber and the produce of their farms was the Mississippi. But Spain, for two hundred miles and more, held both banks of that river. The Spanish government dreaded democracy, and the free-and-easy western boatmen were not at all tender of any one's prejudices. The result was that the Spaniards tried to close the commerce of the river to them, and nearly prevailed upon the weak government of the Confederation to accede to their wishes, when a burst of wrath from beyond the Alleghanies convinced John Jay, the secretary of foreign affairs, that the giving-up of free navigation of the Mississippi would mean the loss of the western territories. In 1795 these disputes were brought to an end by the signing of a treaty at Madrid by which the Spanish government recognized the thirty - first parallel as the southern limit of the United States, between the Mississippi and the Chattahoochee rivers, and agreed to give the citizens of the United States

[1] See McLaughlin, *Confederation and Constitution* (*Am. Nation*, X.), chap· vi.

not only the free navigation of the Mississippi, but "the right of deposit" at New Orleans. This was the right to land their goods free of duty or other payment while awaiting transshipment. Louisiana now suddenly comes within the scope of European politics.[1]

The result of the French Revolution was to bring into power two of the most extraordinary men the world has seen in modern times — Napoleon and Talleyrand. Whether the plan for the resuscitation of the French colonial empire emanated from the abnormal brain of Napoleon Bonaparte or from the equally abnormal brain of Charles Maurice de Talleyrand-Périgord has not been definitely ascertained, nor does it matter for our present purposes. Either of them was quite capable of originating the scheme which threatened to engulf the United States in the vortex of European politics.

The French colony of Santo Domingo "in the good old days," before the fall of the Bastile, was one of the most attractive places of residence for a well-to-do white man in the American sub-tropics. But in 1795 began a revolution and race war in which the negroes of that French colonial paradise killed their masters and mistresses, or such of them as they could reach, and set up a government of their own. The leader of this movement, Toussaint L'Ouverture, Henry Adams likens to a black Napoleon—a kind of "gilded African," to use Napoleon's

[1] See Bassett, *Federalist System* (*Am. Nation*, XI.), chap. v.

own phrase. There is a good deal to be said for the likeness: both were the products of sanguinary revolution, both were faithless despots, both lost their empires, and both died in exile. Napoleon and Talleyrand designed to rebuild the French colonial empire in the east and in the west; with the latter attempt alone are these pages concerned.[1] The idea was to re-establish French rule in Santo Domingo, including therein the re-enslavement of the negroes, to add the Spanish part of the island, which had already been ceded by Spain, but not taken over, to the recovered French portion, and to regain Louisiana from the Spaniards. It will be seen that this plan required the cession of Spanish territory; a glance at the condition of affairs in the Spanish peninsula will therefore be necessary.

Don Carlos, the fourth of the name, then occupied the Spanish throne. The actual rulers in Spain were Doña Maria Luisa de Parma, his queen, and Don Manuel Godoy, el Principe de la Paz, which title writers of English habitually translate Prince of Peace. If Don Carlos was a "good" king, interested mainly in machine - shops and hunting, Luisa of Parma and the Prince of Peace were bad enough to make the average of the three terribly low. Absolutely unscrupulous, as long as the two latter agreed, they completely hoodwinked the lord of the machine-shop and of the kingdom. Bad as he was, Godoy had more than a spark of patriotism.

[1] Adams, *United States*, I., chaps. xiv., xv.

He realized that he was *persona non grata* to the rulers of France, and so he told the king that he must resign. When Napoleon and Talleyrand approached the Spanish monarch with their request for the cession of Louisiana, therefore, the wily Prince of Peace was not at the helm.[1]

The bait which Napoleon and Talleyrand dangled before Don Carlos and Doña Maria Luisa de Parma was nothing less than an Italian kingdom of at least one million inhabitants for the prince - presumptive of Parma, who was at the same time their son-in-law and their nephew. The territory selected was Tuscany, and the title for the new monarch was King of Etruria. For this dignity Spain retroceded Louisiana to France, and further stated that after the general peace the king might also cede that portion of West Florida which lay between the Mississippi and the Mobile. This treaty[2] was signed at San Ildefonso on October 1, 1800; the day before, September 30, the convention of 1800[3] between France and the United States had been signed. As Henry Adams justly remarks, the first of these agreements undid the work of the later.

[1] On the general subject of the plans of Napoleon and Talleyrand, see Adams, *United States*, I., 334–398, and W. M. Sloane, in *Am. Hist. Rev.*, IV., 439.

[2] *Am. State Paps.*, *Public Lands*, VII., 576; De Clercq, *Recueil de Traités de la France*, I., 411.

[3] *Treaties and Conventions*, 266; *Am. State Paps.*, *Public Lands*, V., 711.

CHAPTER V

THE LOUISIANA PURCHASE

(1801–1803)

THE secret of the retrocession of Louisiana was well kept. The first mention of it, in Jefferson's correspondence, was eight months later (May 26, 1801). On that day he wrote to Monroe that "there is considerable reason to apprehend that Spain cedes Louisiana and the Floridas to France." He added that this policy, to his mind, was very unwise for both France and Spain and "very ominous to us."[1]

The first step in the prosecution of the French plans for rebuilding an American colonial empire was the reconquest of Santo Domingo. That island would serve as a sort of stepping-stone between France and Louisiana; moreover, Louisiana would provide a basis of supplies for the laborers of the island. On November 22, 1801, Leclerc, Napoleon's brother-in-law, sailed from Brest for Santo Domingo with ten thousand soldiers. His object was truly stated by Robert R. Livingston, the new American minister at Paris, to be in the first instance Santo

[1] Jefferson, *Writings* (Ford's ed.), VIII., 58.

Domingo, and then, if Toussaint made no opposition, to proceed to Louisiana.

Fortunately for the United States, not only
Toussaint, but half a million Santo Domingo negroes
vindictively opposed the French, and their efforts
to destroy the invading army were most relentlessly
seconded by the yellow-fever. Ten months later,
September, 1802, Leclerc wrote to his brother-in-law
and master that of the 28,000 men who, up to that
time, had been sent to Santo Domingo, 4000 remained
fit for service. In order to enable him to conquer
the island, 12,000 men should be sent to him without
losing a day, to be followed by 5000 more in the next
summer. Instead of subduing the Santo Domingans,
re-establishing slavery and France's colonial empire
in America, General Leclerc himself died within a
month of writing this letter.[1]

Jefferson watched the doings of the French in
Santo Domingo with the keenest anxiety. After the
early successes of Leclerc, and before "yellow jack"
laid hold of the army, Jefferson wrote one of the
most alarmist letters which ever came from his pen.
This was the well-known epistle to Robert R. Livingston, dated at Washington, April 18, 1802.[2] In
this letter the president wrote that every eye in the
United States was now turned to the affair of Louisiana, and that perhaps nothing since the Revolutionary War had produced more uneasy sensations

[1] Adams, *United States*, I., 418.
[2] Jefferson, *Writings* (Ford's ed.), VIII., 143

through the body of the nation. His idea was, although he does not seem to have heard directly from Livingston, that the troops which had been sent to Santo Domingo were to proceed to Louisiana after finishing their work on the island. He thought, however, that this would be no short matter, and would give Livingston time to show the French government the error which they were making. Jefferson argued the subject out somewhat in this wise: (1) the natural feeling of the American people was one of affection towards the French nation, but (2) New Orleans was the one single spot on the globe the possessor of which was the natural and habitual enemy of the American people; (3) as long as this place remained in the possession of Spain, it did not matter, for Spain was well-disposed to the United States and was at best a feeble and declining power; (4) France, on the other hand, possessed an energy and restlessness of character which would bring about eternal friction with the United States. "The day that France takes possession of N. Orleans fixes the sentence which is to restrain her forever within her low water mark," declared Jefferson. "It seals the union of two nations who in conjunction can maintain exclusive possession of the ocean. From that moment we must marry ourselves to the British fleet and nation. . . . The first cannon, which shall be fired in Europe, [will be] the signal for tearing up any settlement she may have made, and for holding the two continents of

America in sequestration for the common purposes of the united British and American nations." This was not an end which America desired, he declared, but the possession of Louisiana by France would force her to it. When we consider that this letter was written by the author of the *Summary View* and of the Declaration of Independence, we may get an idea of the degree to which the mind of Thomas Jefferson was stirred.

In November, 1802, news reached Washington that the Spanish authorities at New Orleans had suddenly withdrawn the right of deposit.[1] The western country at once burst into flame. The Federalists, overjoyed at this outflare on the part of Jefferson's sturdy western supporters, sought, by making the most frantic appeals for instant war, to compel the president to take some rash and ill-considered step or lose the aid of the Democrats of Kentucky and Tennessee. Never in all his long and varied career did Jefferson's foxlike discretion stand him in better stead. Instead of following the public clamor, he calmly formulated a policy and carried it through to a most successful termination.

The first thing to do was to quiet the public mind; the second thing was to regain the right of

[1] Laussat, Napoleon's agent in the transfer of Louisiana to the United States, reported that the right of deposit was withdrawn by the Spanish governor, Salcedo, against the advice of Morales, contrary to the usual statement. See Villiers du Terrage, *Les Dernières Années de la Louisiane Française*, 367.

deposit; the third thing was to steer a tortuous course between France and England and to take advantage of every possible opening to secure possession of New Orleans and the Gulf coast, and in this way to put an end forever to all chances of similar trouble in the future.

To quiet the public mind, Jefferson adopted a calm tone, as if nothing in the world had happened. In his second annual message[1] to Congress, December, 1802, he observed that the cession of Louisiana to France, if carried into effect, would make a change in the aspect of our foreign relations, but what that change would be he did not say. In the middle of January, 1803, General Samuel Smith moved that the House proceed to executive session. When the floors and galleries were cleared, he moved to appropriate two million dollars "to defray any expenses in relation to the intercourse between the United States and foreign nations." On the same day Jefferson nominated James Monroe, of Virginia, as minister-extraordinary to France and Spain. The appropriation was made and the nomination was confirmed. On January 13, 1803, Jefferson wrote to Monroe, explaining to him the reason for his appointment.[2] In this letter the president states that the Federalists were trying to force the administration into war, or, if this could not be done, to attach the western country to them and ride into

---

[1] Richardson, *Messages and Papers*, I., 342.
[2] Jefferson, *Writings* (Ford's ed.), VIII., 190.

power on the crest of the wave of popular up-
heaval. Something "sensible," by which Jefferson
undoubtedly meant something that could be sensed
or observed, was necessary. He therefore had selected Monroe to go to France to act with the
resident minister there. So successful, indeed, had
been this policy that the Federalists in Washington were already silenced. Jefferson lamented the
necessity for this entanglement in European politics,
because the United States, although making a larger
figure, would be much less happy and prosperous.

The French and British diplomatic agents at
Washington at once bestirred themselves to dis-
cover what was in the mind of the administration.
Thornton,[1] the British *chargé*, wrote to the British
foreign minister, Lord Hawkesbury, that he doubted
the administration would take such a measure of
vigor as would place the United States on commanding ground with Spain and eventually with
France. Jefferson,[2] however, told Thornton, according to the latter's note of January 31, 1803, that
the country would never abandon the claim to the
free navigation of the Mississippi; that, on the
whole, he thought it very probable that Monroe
might be obliged to cross the Channel to England,
and that the United States, if compelled to resort to
force, would throw away the scabbard. Pichon,
the French *chargé*, was also thoroughly stirred up.

[1] Adams, *United States*, I., 430, from the British archives.
[2] *Ibid.*, 436, from the British archives.

He wrote to Talleyrand [1] that it was impossible for a government to be more bitter than that of the United States, and that Mr. Jefferson would be forced to yield to necessity his scruples against a British alliance. "I noticed," wrote Pichon, "at his table that he redoubled his civilities and attentions to the British *chargé*." To make the matter certain, Madison sent for Pichon and explained to him that the possession of New Orleans and West Florida was a necessity for the Americans. New Orleans was of no value to the French: they could sell it to the Americans and build another city on the opposite bank of the river.

Even Gallatin talked of war, and Monroe told Pichon that the administration would act with the utmost vigor, that it might be compelled to receive the overtures of England, and that if the tie were once made between England and the United States they would not stop half-way. [2] Altogether, everything was done to make the French understand that the question at issue was either to let go their hold on Louisiana or to witness the marriage between the United States and Great Britain. In April, 1803, Madison wrote to Livingston and Monroe that if the French government should meditate hostilities or force a war with the United States, by closing the Mississippi to commerce, that they were to invite England to make an alliance which should

[1] Adams, *United States*, I., 437, from the French archives.
[2] *Ibid.*, 440, from the French archives.

bind the United States and Great Britain to make no treaty or truce without the consent of the other party. While Madison still had these instructions on his desk, the Spanish minister at Washington walked into his office and told him that his government had sent a special messenger to inform the president that the right of deposit would be restored, and to thank the American magistrate for his friendly conduct in the recent time of excitement. In this way Jefferson's peace policy achieved its first triumph.[1]

Meantime, affairs had been moving rapidly in France, as was their wont in those days. Napoleon, irritated by the constant failure in Santo Domingo, suddenly turned in anger and loathing from colonial enterprises. With one of those abrupt face-abouts which he may have learned at the military school, he now seemed to be as solicitous to rid himself of Louisiana as he had been anxious a few months earlier to secure it. Louisiana was of no use without Santo Domingo, and Santo Domingo could not be conquered with any means at his command. America could be conquered in Europe much more easily than it could be in America. Napoleon's prestige had been injured by the many disasters to French arms in Santo Domingo; it must be regained by one or more brilliant strokes at home. Besides, Louisiana could not be held for a moment in case of war, if the United States alone should undertake its seiz-

[1] Adams, *United States*, II., 3.

ure. Still less could it be held if the American people, in conjunction with the British fleet and nation, should undertake its conquest. Besides, Napoleon, with a Frenchman's idea of things maritime, dreaded—or detested would perhaps be the better word—the sea-power of Great Britain. In the cession of Louisiana to the United States his prophetic eye, peering far into the future, saw the young republic become a world-power, alone among nations able to lower the pride of the Mistress of the Seas.[1] It would be well, however, to make as much money out of the matter as possible. Fifty millions of francs would go far towards restoring the self-love of France—somewhat damaged in Santo Domingo. Besides, the money would come in handy in fitting out a naval force for the invasion of the hated Albion or an army for the conquest of a kingdom or a duchy or two in Germany. The fact that he had promised Don Carlos not to alienate Louisiana to any foreign power does not seem to have occurred to Napoleon, or, if it did occur to him, it does not appear to have been regarded as of the slightest moment. Probably it never once crossed his mind—except as one of those ugly facts which would be better dismissed as soon as possible.

Sending for Marbois, for he probably hesitated to trust Talleyrand with the handling of the money, Napoleon ordered him to see Livingston, then sole minister at Paris, that very day, and make arrange-

[1] Barbé-Marbois, *Histoire de la Louisiane*, 282.

ments for the sale of the colony—New Orleans and
all the rest. Talleyrand, cognizant of Napoleon's decision, was the first, however, to break the matter to
Livingston.[1]

Robert R. Livingston, of New York, is one of the
few great Americans whose life remains to be written.
With Jefferson he served on that famous committee
of five which drew up the Declaration of Independence, or, to speak more accurately perhaps, authorized Jefferson to draw it up. Later, Livingston
acted as chancellor of New York, and in that capacity administered the oath of office to the first president of the United States. Age, however, was a
constitutional disqualification for the chancellor-
ship in New York. Livingston, therefore, entered
the service of the United States on the coming into
power of his old friend, and was appointed minister
to France. For weeks he had been dancing atten-
dance on Talleyrand, seeking to buy the island of
Orleans and West Florida. Suddenly, on Monday,
April 11, 1803, the very day on which Napoleon
had placed the negotiation in Marbois's hands, Talleyrand startled Livingston by asking him whether
the United States wished to have the whole of
Louisiana? Livingston said No; that the United
States had in mind only New Orleans and the
Floridas; but he thought, in addition, that France
might very well sell Louisiana above the Arkansas,
as that region was of no use to her. Talleyrand

[1] *Am. State Paps., Foreign*, II., 552.

replied by the observation that without New Orleans
Louisiana itself would be of no use to France, and
wanted to know what the United States would give
for the whole thing? Livingston replied that it
was a subject he had not thought of, but that he
supposed that the Americans would not object to
twenty millions of francs, provided France paid the
claims of the citizens of the United States for French
spoliations since the period covered by the convention of 1800. Talleyrand replied that this sum
was too little. Livingston closed the interview by
saying that he would think the matter over, that
Monroe would reach Paris within a short time and
that the two of them would then make a further
offer. The next day Livingston and Talleyrand had
another conversation, but without result. That afternoon Monroe reached Paris, but it was Wednes-
day evening before Marbois opened the matter. He
invited Livingston to his house, and in a midnight
conversation the two settled the business.[1] Monroe
had not then been received as minister. The formal
conduct of the negotiation fell to Livingston, who
was well known and liked by Marbois. The next
few days were spent in haggling over the price. Marbois proposed one hundred and twenty-five millions
of francs—although Napoleon, as we know, had told
him to sell it for fifty millions. Finally, the negotiators settled on the sum of eighty millions of francs,

[1] For Monroe's account of the negotiations, see *Writings*,
VI., 10.

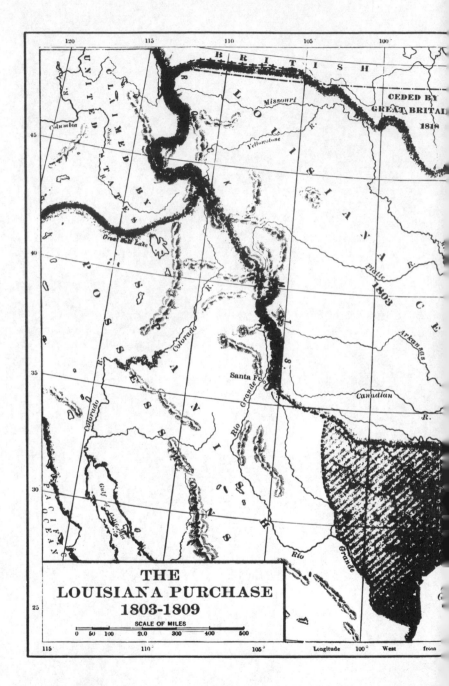

THE
LOUISIANA PURCHASE
1803-1809

SCALE OF MILES

0   50   100   200   300   400   500

sixty of them to go to France direct, the rest to be
paid by the United States to American citizens in
the settlement of claims against France — fifteen
million dollars in all. Such was the price paid for
an empire, the western half of the most valuable
river valley on the surface of the earth.

It took three weeks to put all the various matters
into shape. Monroe was formally received by Napoleon on May 1, and on May 2 the treaty of cession was actually signed.[1] After Livingston set his
name to the great act, he rose and, shaking hands
with Monroe and Marbois, said, "We have lived
long, but this is the noblest work of our lives."
What Livingston said was true, for without the
Louisiana purchase the United States would not
have grown into the strong nation which it has
since become. To Napoleon, also, the cession seemed full of promise: "Sixty millions for an occupation that will not last perhaps a day."

The most curious thing about the Louisiana purchase, however, is to be found in the fact to which
Napoleon alluded, that France was able to hand
over to the United States an imperial domain which
was not in her possession and which, indeed, she had
no right to sell to the United States. In the first

---

[1] Monroe was not formally received until May 1; the treaties
were signed on May 2 and 8 or 9, but were all antedated to
April 30, on which day the French copy of the principal treaty
was completed. See *Am. State Paps., Foreign*, II., 507. The
treaties are in *Treaties and Conventions between the United States
and other Powers*, 275–282.

place, Napoleon had promised the Spaniards that France would not alienate Louisiana, that if she did not occupy it herself she would restore the province to Spain. In the second place, it cannot be said that Napoleon had ever fulfilled the condition on which Louisiana had been retroceded to France. Finally, the constitution of the French republic forbade the executive by his own power to dispose of the dominions of France. The measure of credit which can attach to Livingston and Monroe, to Jefferson and Madison, is not hard to see. 'Diplomatically, they had achieved nothing; Louisiana had been thrown into their hands through no efforts of theirs. Great credit is due to them, nevertheless, because, when the fate of the United States hung in the balance, they took the responsibility of paying money, millions of dollars, which they had no authority to expend in the purchase of the country which they had no authority to buy. In after years the New England Federalists, with an obliquity of vision peculiar to themselves, hinted that this transaction was a mask to hide the payment of tribute to France![1]

[1] *Address to the People of the County of Hampshire* [Mass.] *in 1809*, 7.

CHAPTER VI

THE ADMINISTRATION OF LOUISIANA

(1803–1812)

WHEN the news of the purchase of Louisiana for fifteen million dollars reached the United States, Jefferson was thunderstruck. It was not the expenditure of the money which troubled him, it was not the acquisition of an empire which disturbed his mind, it was the constitutional aspect which annoyed him, but which, curiously enough, did not in the least trouble his strict-constructionist adherents in Kentucky and Tennessee.

For years Jefferson and his followers had been talking about the necessity of interpreting the Constitution with the greatest strictness. But where in that instrument could they find power expressly delegated to the central government to acquire territory? That troubled Jefferson, because he felt that what he was doing was for the good of the nation, and that the nation would ratify his act, and in so doing would make the Constitution so much blank paper. But this seemed to be the only thing that could be done. In a letter to John

Breckinridge,[1] dated Monticello, August 12, 1803, Jefferson likens himself to a guardian who has invested the money of his ward in purchasing an important estate, and saying to his ward, when he has come of age: "I did this for your good; I pretend to no right to bind you; you may disavow me, and I must get out of the scrape as I can; I thought it my duty to risk myself for you."[2] But Jefferson felt that he would not be disavowed by the nation, that the nation would confirm his act, and by an amendment to the Constitution at once justify him and strengthen that instrument.

Acting on this general idea, the president drew up amendments to the Constitution.[3] At first Jefferson was inclined to incorporate the province of Louisiana in the Union with a strict guarantee of the rights of the Indians. In another draft, the district north of the Arkansas River is reserved absolutely to the Indians. The reason for this reservation was the clamor which the Federalists made about the new territory draining off the inhabitants from the old settled parts of the Union. Between August 12 and August 18, however, two letters came from Robert R. Livingston, advising the administration to make the greatest despatch, as Napoleon might change his mind at any moment. Jefferson thereupon sat himself down and wrote to his inti-

[1] Jefferson, *Writings* (Ford's ed.), VIII., 244.
[2] *Ibid.*, 244 *n.*
[3] *Ibid.*, 241–249 and notes.

mates[1] that the less said about the constitutional
difficulties the better, and that whatever was done
would better be done in silence. Early in September, Jefferson received a letter from one of his
steadiest and ablest supporters, Wilson Cary Nicholas,[2] which would have done credit to the most
strenuous Federalist of them all. Nicholas wrote
that the Constitution did not in any way confine
the Congress of the United States, in the admission
of new states, to what was at that time the territory
of the United States; it only said that new states
could not be formed out of old ones without the
consent of the state to be dismembered. Nor did
Nicholas see anything in the Constitution that limited the treaty - making power. He acknowledged
that this was delicate ground and might clash
with the opinions which had been held by the
opponents of Jay's treaty; but, nevertheless, he
begged the president to keep to himself his opinion
that the treaty was beyond the power of the government to make, for if that idea once got abroad
the Senate would certainly reject the treaty. So
the treaty was ratified and the Jeffersonian theory
of strict construction was abandoned in the house
of its friends.

The phrase in the treaty defining the limits of
Louisiana was copied from the treaty of San Ilde-

---

[1] Jefferson, *Writings* (Ford's ed.), VIII., 245 *n.*
[2] Adams, *United States*, II., 87, from *Jefferson MSS.* in the
state department.

fonso: "The colony or province of Louisiana, with the same extent that it now has in the hands of Spain, and that it had when France possessed it, and such as it should be after the treaties subsequently entered into between Spain and other states." The territory so described the French republic ceded to the United States as fully and in the same manner as it had been acquired by that republic. The ink on the treaty was scarcely dry when Livingston and Monroe began to ask themselves, and also the French authorities, as to what land it was which they had bought. They got little comfort from the Frenchmen. "You have made a grand bargain," said Talleyrand; "make the most of it"; and Marbois, when it was suggested that the boundaries were indefinite, said that they were, and that if the language had not been indefinite it would have been well to have made it so.[1] From that time to this there has been constant disputation over this matter. While the treaty was forming, Livingston and Monroe seemed to have understood that what they were buying did not include any part of what was then called the Floridas. But no sooner was the treaty signed than they made up their minds that the sale included as much of West Florida as had at one time formed a part of French Louisiana. It was easy to base an argument for this on the phrase "extent that it had when France possessed it." Monroe, indeed, was for setting off

[1] Barbé-Marbois, *Histoire de la Louisiane*, 311.

post-haste to Spain to complete the purchase of the
Floridas, but he was discouraged from taking this
journey by Cambacérès, who acted as Napoleon's
colleague, with the title of consul, and also by Talleyrand. As a matter of fact, the government at
Madrid was so excessively irritated by the action of
Napoleon in selling that which did not belong to him,
and which he had promised never to sell, that there
is no telling what they might have done had Monroe
appeared at Madrid with the statement in one hand
that Florida, to the Perdido River, or the Perdigo
River, as he sometimes spelled it, had been sold
by France to the United States, and that he would
like to buy the remainder of Florida for a million
or two.

Even more interesting has been the question
whether Louisiana included Texas.[1] For sixteen
years 'this formed a subject of negotiation. Later
on it justified in part the absorption of Texas into
the United States, and nowadays it is giving rise
to an interesting debate between historical students
throughout the country, and also between what
might be termed historico - politicians in Texas
and Louisiana. The Louisianians appear to regard
the Texans as interlopers. The Texans, on the
other hand, appear to be disposed to claim that
Texas was a part of the great purchase, and also
later achieved its independence from Mexico. Jef-

[1] Jefferson stated his ideas as to the limits of Louisiana in a
paper printed in *Jefferson-Dunbar Documents*, No. 1.

ferson, Madison, Monroe, and John Quincy Adams maintained that Texas was an integral part of Louisiana when France possessed that province, that such possession as Spain had of a few mission stations was in the nature of what the lawyers call "adverse possession." Into the historical subtilties of this argument it is not at all necessary to go. When the French government prepared the instructions for General Victor, who was expected to take over the colony from the Spaniards, it declared that Louisiana was bounded on the west by the river called Rio Bravo, which we now call the Rio Grande, from its mouth to about the thirtieth degree. From that point, the instructions stated, no agreement had been reached as to the line of demarcation.[1] Victor, as it turned out, did not go to Louisiana; but the instructions were turned over to Laussat, who acted under them.

This clause in Victor's instructions seems to Mr. Henry Adams conclusive proof that Jefferson, Madison, Monroe, and John Quincy Adams were justified in their belief that Louisiana extended to the Rio Grande. Against this view have been urged legal and historical arguments with great show of

[1] Adams, *United States*, II., 6, from the French Archives de la Marine. See also Madison to Livingston, March 31, 1804, *Am. State Paps., Foreign*, II., 575. According to this letter, it appears that Laussat, at the time of the formal handing over of Louisiana, had repeated this clause in the instructions which he had received. For a contrary view, see J. R. Ficklen, in Southern History Association, *Publications*, September, 1901.

learning and fortified with references to historical maps. The whole history of the transference of Louisiana from Spain to the United States through the medium of France is so absolutely opposed to legal and historical hypotheses that it seems quite useless to argue the matter on any such grounds. It is perfectly clear that Napoleon had no right to sell Louisiana, legally or otherwise; he did not even have that possession which is sometimes supposed to make good other defects. Of what use, then, is it to spend time in legal niceties? Napoleon sold us Louisiana, and we became possessed of Louisiana, simply and solely because he held the Spanish monarchy by the throat. Whatever he meant to take possession of under the name of Louisiana, he intended to hand over to us and handed over to us. In taking Louisiana we were the accomplices of the greatest highwayman of modern history, and the goods which we received were those which he compelled his unwilling victim to disgorge.

When the Louisiana treaty came before Congress, speeches were made in both Houses which ought to have caused a blush of shame to mantle the cheek of even the egotistical John Randolph of Roanoke. In the Kentucky Resolutions of 1798, introduced and defended by John Breckinridge, the Kentucky legislature had declared itself determined "tamely to submit to undelegated, and consequently unlimited, powers in no man or body of men on earth." Now Senator Breckinridge maintained that foreign territory could actually be admitted into the Union as a state or any number of states by treaty. Africa, for instance, Breckinridge admitted, containing more inhabitants than the whole United States, might be incorporated by treaty in the Union, even to the destruction of the government.[1] The true construction of the Constitution must depend, among other things, on the good sense of the community. In other words, a president and two-thirds of the Senate, by the exercise of the treaty-making power, could do anything they saw fit.

The question as to the immediate government of the new acquisition was settled in a way which one would scarcely have dreamed a Jeffersonian Congress could have brought itself to adopt. By an act[2] of Congress the government of the new territory was placed absolutely in the hands of the president of the United States, who simply stepped into the shoes of the king of Spain, so far as Louisiana was concerned. To the Federalist objection that the powers conferred on the president by this bill were unconstitutional, Cæsar A. Rodney, of Delaware, replied that Congress had a power in the territories which they had not in the states, and that the limitations of the Constitution were applicable to the states and not to the territories.[3] Over lands and

[1] *Annals of Cong.*, 8 Cong., 1 Sess., 63.
[2] *Laws of the United States*, VII., 2 (Acts of 1 Sess. of 8 Cong., chap. i.); *U. S. Statutes at Large*, II., 245.
[3] *Annals of Cong.*, 8 Cong. 1 Sess., 513.

over people which the United States might acquire by treaty — whether the consent of those people was asked or not — the government of the United States possessed as absolute a power as the most tyrannical despot in Christendom or Heathenesse. By a subsequent act, the southern part of the territory, that portion which afterwards formed the state of Louisiana — omitting the bit of the state east of the island of Orleans—was formed into the territory of Orleans under a government like that of the first territorial stage under the Northwest Ordinance.[1] That territorial stage had been designed for a region practically without inhabitants; the new territory of Orleans contained at the moment fifty thousand human beings, of whom more than half were negro slaves.

The treaty was signed April 30, 1803, but it was the 30th of the following November before Napoleon's agent, Laussat, received possession of the province from the Count of Casa Calvo, the Spanish governor. Seventeen days later (December 17, 1803), William C. C. Claiborne received possession of the province for the government of the United States.[2] These dates have a certain interest as emphasizing the fact that Napoleon did not have possession of Louisiana when he sold it to the United

[1] *Laws of the United States*, VII., 112–136 (Acts of 1 Sess. of 8 Cong., chap. xxxviii.); *U. S. Statutes at Large*, II., 283.

[2] Documents regarding the transfer to France and again to the United States are in *Am. State Paps.*, *Public Lands*, V., 708, 727, etc.; VII., 578.

States, or even, for that matter, when the ratifications of the treaty were exchanged at Washington. Brief as was the French occupation, it continued long enough for Laussat to publish a new code of French law which reproduced many of the principles of the Code Napoleon. The principal result of this speed in giving laws to a province which was already sold was to make more confused than before the confusion of the combined French law of the old régime and the Spanish laws of the Indies. In due time the new American masters introduced the English language and many English legal institutions, as, for example, trial by jury. Judge Martin, in his *History of Louisiana*, relates that there were three sets of interpreters employed in the courts of the territory. These confined their efforts to the evidence and the charge of the judge; it was not thought necessary to translate the arguments of the lawyers. The results were sometimes such as to make the new French and Spanish subjects of the United States entertain a certain amount of distrust of American justice. This feeling was not at all allayed by the inrush of pioneer lawyers who had great energy, slight knowledge of American law, and no knowledge whatever of French Napoleonic or monarchical institutions, or of the laws of the Indies. Nevertheless, these men saw the opportunity to make money. They bought up claims to lands and fought them through the polyglot courts of the territory and, later, of the state. There is

one exception to the general remark as to the ignorance of the carpet-bag members of the legal
fraternity.   Edward Livingston, brother of the ne-
gotiator of the treaty, became involved in serious
difficulties in New York, owing to carelessness in
the management of the government money which
passed through his hands.[1]   He emigrated to Louisiana, where he won eternal reputation by combining
the various legal practices which prevailed in Louisiana into one code which is always cited by his name
and is still the basis of the legal institutions of that
region.[2]

In the autumn of 1804, the territorial government of Louisiana was organized with William C.
C. Claib- ne as governor.   Coupled with this new
organization,[3] in which there was not the slightest
vestige of the representative principle, there was the
further provision that no slaves should be carried
thither except from some part of the United States,
and then only by American citizens removing into
the territory as actual settlers, and even these might
not carry with them slaves who had been imported since 1798.   This extreme squeamishness on the
part of a Republican Congress which was dominated by southern interest was due to the excitement that had arisen over the repeal by South

[1] See C. H. Hunt, *Life of Edward Livingston* (1864), 101.
[2] *Ibid.*, chap. xii.
[3] *Laws of the United States*, VII., 112 (Acts of 1 Sess. of 8 Cong.,
chap. xxxviii., § 10); *U. S. Statutes at Large*, II., 286.

Carolina of the state law prohibiting the importation of blacks. As the conditions of cultivation in Louisiana were not unlike those which prevailed in South Carolina, this prohibition on the importation of blacks would have been severely felt by Governor Claiborne's new subjects had the restriction continued for any length of time. The Louisianians petitioned Congress for relief, and most of the restrictions were removed at an early date. In the event it was perhaps fortunate that more slaves were not imported into the colony, for in 1811 a most dangerous insurrection began in the parish of St John the Baptist, which is situated not far above New Orleans. About five hundred negroes armed themselves and started on their march for New Orleans, burning plantations and massacring the planters and their families as they proceeded. United States troops and militia finally put down the uprising. To deter any negroes in the future from seeking to gain their liberty, the heads of the leaders of this plot were displayed on poles along the banks of the river.[1]

The inhabitants of the part of old Louisiana situated to the east of the lakes and the river became more and more restive as the years went by and the Spanish government refused to sell them and their land to the United States. In 1805 they rebelled against their Spanish masters, but were defeated. In July, 1810, however, they tried again;

[1] Martin, *History of Louisiana*, II., 301.

this time they drove out the Spanish garrison at Baton Rouge, held a convention, and declared West Florida to be a free and independent state. Madison seized the opportunity to annex to the United States as a part of the Louisiana purchase so much of the region as was not in Spanish hands. By presidential proclamation of October 27, 1810, he added the new territory to the territory of Orleans.[1] At the time this possession only extended to the Pearl River, but in 1813 Wilkinson occupied Mobile. From this time on the remainder of the old Louisiana as far as the Perdido River may be considered as in the possession of the United States. In 1812 the state of Louisiana, with its present boundaries, was admitted to the Union,[2] Claiborne becoming the first elected governor of the new state.

[1] Richardson, *Messages and Papers*, I., 480.   Some original matter as to the rebellion is printed in *Am. Hist. Rev.*, II., 699.
[2] *Laws of the United States of America*, XI., 95 (Acts of 1 Sess. of 12 Cong., chap. 1.); *U. S. Statutes at Large*, II., 701.

CHAPTER VII

THE EXPLORATION OF THE WEST
(1803–1806)

JEFFERSON'S scientific inclinations had led him, long before his election to the presidency, to take an interest in western exploration.[1] An expedition into the region west of the Mississippi would add to the total sum of human knowledge, it would bring back to civilization descriptions of the fauna and the flora of that country, of its geography, and might possibly announce to the world the discovery of the remains of some unsuspected extinct animal. Such an expedition might also open the way for American tradesmen and trappers in competition with Frenchmen and Englishmen. Years before, while American minister at Paris, Jefferson had encouraged the wild project of the eccentric John Ledyard to journey around the world from Europe eastward through Asiatic Russia, Siberia, across the Pacific to Alaska, and thence through the unknown parts of North America. Ledyard set out on this journey, but was finally

[1] See Jefferson, *Writings* (Ford's ed.), VI., 158; VIII., 192 *n*.

turned back by the Russians when on the confines of Kamchatka. In 1792, while secretary of state, Jefferson returned to the project of the exploration of the country west of the Mississippi. This time two men were to attempt the feat. These were Meriwether Lewis, a young Virginian of adventurous disposition, and André Michaux, a French savant of some reputation. The latter was recalled, and the expedition was a failure.

When Jefferson became president he appointed Lewis as his private secretary, and it was not long before they had contrived a new scheme for an exploration on a much larger scale than anything hitherto contemplated. In January, 1803, in the crisis of the excitement over the withdrawal of the right of deposit, Jefferson sent a message to Congress[1] adverting to the ignorance which prevailed concerning the Indians of the Missouri, which was undesirable in view of "their connection with the Mississippi and consequently with us." He therefore proposed that an intelligent officer, with ten or twelve chosen men taken from the ranks of the army, should explore even to the western ocean. The extra expense beyond their pay and rations would be a bonus of land to each man and twenty-five hundred dollars to be expended in scientific instruments and "light and cheap presents for the

---

[1] Richardson, *Messages and Papers*, I., 352. The instructions to Lewis and Clark are in Jefferson, *Writings* (Ford's ed.), VIII., 194 *n.*

Indians." The president nowhere alludes in so many words to the fact that he was proposing to Congress to authorize him to send a detachment of the United States army into the territory of a friendly state; but he seems to recognize the equivocal character of the enterprise by suggesting that Congress pass a bill appropriating the sum asked for to extend the external commerce of the United States. This form "would cover the undertaking from notice and prevent the obstructions which interested individuals might otherwise previously prepare in its way." Undoubtedly if Spain had set on foot an expedition to explore the waters of the Illinois in the interests of her external commerce, and the matter had come to the attention of the American government, obstructions would have previously been prepared in its way. The Louisiana purchase came in the nick of time to save Jefferson from violating the code of international ethics. Whether the expedition was planned partly with a view to possible seizure of the country cannot be stated; the conjunction of dates is remarkable.[1]

The command of the expedition which was set on foot in consequence of the favorable action of Congress was given to Meriwether Lewis, William Clark being joined with him. Clark was a younger brother of George Rogers Clark of Revolutionary fame.

[1] The message nominating Monroe minister to France and Spain was dated January 11, 1803; that as to this expedition, January 18. Richardson, *Messages and Papers*, I., 350, 352.

They possessed adventurous spirits and fidelity to their trust and to each other, which have made the names of Lewis and Clark inseparable from each other and from the history of the country which they were the first men of European stock to traverse. At the moment Clark was not in the army, but he was given a commission as lieutenant. Lewis already had a commission as captain in the army. Both of them had seen service in the Indian campaigns of the preceding decade. They raised a force of picked men, some from the ranks of the enlisted men of the army, others taken from private life, but regularly enlisted in the military service. The expedition was carried on under the articles of war; months—half a year, in fact—were devoted to hardening the men to rigid discipline. To this preparation much of the success of the expedition was due. Seldom in history has a body of more highly trained frontier fighters been launched into the wilderness.

In May, 1804, the expedition left its winter-quarters on the bank of the river Du Bois, which falls into the Mississippi from the Illinois side about a day's journey from St. Louis. There were forty-five persons in all, in three boats. One of these was a batteau, or flat-boat, fifty-five feet in length and decked at the ends; the others were keel-boats called pirogues[1] in the language of the time and place. The boats were propelled by oars, setting-poles, or

[1] Coues, *Lewis and Clark Expedition*, I., 4 *n*.

sails, as occasion served. The rapid and uncertain current of the Missouri, the ever-recurring shallows, and the violent and changeable winds combined to make progress slow and difficult. For a time, also, the expedition was held back by the necessity of awaiting the arrival of horses, which were driven along the river's bank for the use of the hunters. The amount of game, large and small, was prodigious; until the mountains were reached the expedition was abundantly supplied with food. For the greater part of their journey up-stream the Indians were conspicuous by their absence. When they did appear they were friendly, or, at all events, not hostile. In the whole course of their upward journey their one unpleasant experience was with a band of the Sioux;) but the firm hand and resolute bearing of the young leaders and the well-trained men at their back daunted even the Sioux, and no open attack was made. Higher up the river, near the site of Bismarck, North Dakota, they came to the Mandans, who dwelt in villages of permanent wigwams. Not far from the site of one of these aboriginal towns the voyagers settled down for the winter and wrote up their journals and observations with assiduous care. At this place they happened upon an Indian squaw, the so-called Bird Woman, who belonged to one of the mountain tribes, and had been kidnapped years before. She and her husband, a half-breed, accompanied the expedition when it set forth in the spring of 1805. On the

other hand, a detachment returned down the river
carrying reports of the progress of the expedition up
to that time.

Proceeding onward, the explorers reached the falls
of the Missouri, in Montana. They constructed a
wheeled vehicle on which the lighter of the supplies and impedimenta could be transported around
the obstruction. Here a great disappointment be-
fell Lewis. He had brought from the United States,
at cost of great trouble, the iron frame - work of
a boat. Over this he caused skins to be stretch-
ed; when made, the boat could be easily lifted
and carried by a few men. But it would not float.
They burned trees for pitch, but the pitch would not
come. Finally they had recourse to a combination
of powdered charcoal, beeswax, and buffalo tallow.
The boat floated well enough, but as soon as it was
taken out of the water to dry the mixture dropped off
and left the seams open.[1] After this ending, Lewis
buried the boat-frame and set to work to build
canoes after the Indian style. Again voyaging
upward, the explorers came to a point where the
river forked into three branches. To these they
gave the names of Jefferson, Madison, and Gallatin;
three affluents of the Jefferson they named Philosophy, Philanthropy, and Wisdom; the names of
the principal branches remain, but the subsidiary
streams have lost their pristine appellations, the

[1] *Original Journals of Lewis and Clark Expedition* (Thwaites's
ed.), II., 218.

Philanthropy being now known as Stinking Water. Some preliminary exploration was necessary before they could determine which was the most available route. Finally, with the good-fortune which marked their geographical work, they pitched upon the Jefferson as the proper stream to follow. Laboriously ascending it, they came ere long to a point where it was too shallow for further navigation, even in their canoes. Lewis then set out overland, seeking the Indians of the mountains. These proved to be shy. Finally he succeeded in surprising an old woman and some girls. The women held down their heads for instant execution. Instead, Lewis gave them beads and trinkets, and painted their faces with vermilion in token of amity. At this moment the men of the tribe rode up. After much patient endeavor and some hunger, Lewis persuaded some of them to go with him to the river, where the Indian woman who had accompanied them was recognized as sister of the chief of the band[1] upon which the explorers had so opportunely chanced.

Dangers and hardships now fast accumulated. Wild animals were no longer abundant, and other food was scarce. The waters of the nearest western-flowing river were only three-quarters of a mile from the Jefferson, but the river was full of rocks and the land route to the point where it was navigable was nearly impassable. But there was no

[1] *Original Journals of Lewis and Clark Expedition* (Thwaites's ed.), II., 361.

thought of turning back with their task half done.
They bought horses of the Indians and set out overland. When the river became passable they made
canoes and voyaged down its waters to the Columbia,
and down that stream, encountering hunger, rap-
ids, and whirlpools. On November 7, 1805, in the
distance they came "in *view* of the *Ocian*, this great
Pacific Octean which we have been so long anxious
to See. and the rorcing or noise made by the waves
brakeing on the rockey Shores (as I suppose) may
be heard distictly."[1] So Clark wrote, with a disregard of the niceties of spelling that gives a flavor to
all his "wrightings."

The explorers were destined to hear more of the
waves than they wished. To get near game, and
away from the most thievish of the natives of the
lower Columbia, they voyaged in their canoes along
the coast and landed through the breakers without losing a man. There, on the shore, they built
huts, naming their post Fort Clatsop, from the least
objectionable natives around them. The situation
was uncomfortable, owing to the constant wind and
rain and snow. Especially the lack of adventure
wore upon them, accustomed as they were to an
active life. But everything has an ending. In
March, 1806, the explorers started on their return
journey. The rapid downpouring current of the
river could not be breasted except in its lower

[1] *Original Journals of Lewis and Clark Expedition* (Thwaites's
ed.), III., 210.

course. They were forced to march overland. In due season they reached the village of the friendly Nez Percé Indians, where they had left their horses, and found that these had been kept carefully for them. Obtaining guides, they made a perilous passage across the "Great Divide." They then separated into three parties, to make a more careful exploration. Uniting near the confluence of the Yellowstone and the Missouri, they drifted, rowed, and sailed down that stream until at about noon of September 23, 1806, they arrived at St. Louis.[1] They had performed a feat without parallel in the history of exploration. During all this time of danger, hardship, and exposure one man had deserted, one man had died, one Indian had been killed. The constancy and courage of Lewis and Clark and their companions reflect credit on the leaders and on the men. Their journals read like a romance. Floods, grizzly bears, landslips, and rattlesnakes abounded, but the most dreaded foes were mosquitoes and flies. These pests sometimes beset them night and day, and cast into the background the convulsions of nature, the onslaughts of wild beasts, the peril from Indians. On first viewing the Rockies near at hand, Lewis was for the moment filled with foreboding; but he wrote in his journal that as he had always "held it a crime to antici-

---

[1] The home journey is described in vols. IV. and V. of the Thwaites edition of the *Original Journals of the Lewis and Clark Expedition.*

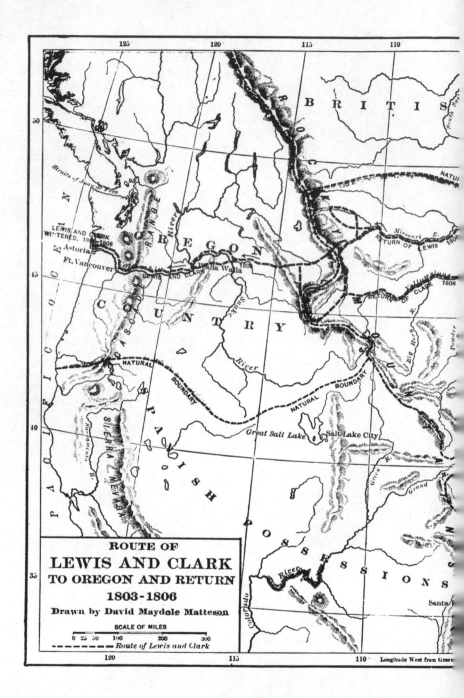

ROUTE OF
LEWIS AND CLARK
TO OREGON AND RETURN
1803-1806
Drawn by David Maydole Matteson

SCALE OF MILES

0 25 50   100   200   300

- - - - - - - Route of Lewis and Clark

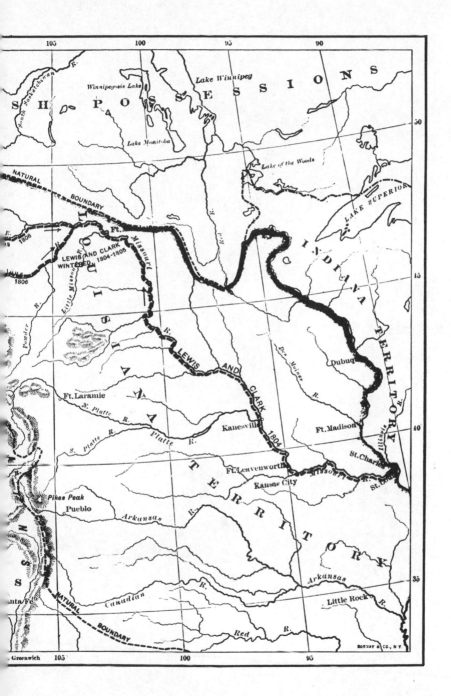

pate evils I will believe it a good comfortable road until I am compelled to believe differently."[1]   It was in this spirit that Lewis and Clark and their men did their work and earned their place in the annals of the United States.

In 1805, while Lewis and Clark were far away in the west, General James Wilkinson sent Lieutenant Zebulon Montgomery Pike to the headwaters of the Mississippi to explore its course, notice places for fortified posts, make peace between Indian tribes, and report on the country through which the river passed.   It is possible that he was sent on this errand at the suggestion of the president, but no hint of this is to be found in the records.[2]   Setting out with a detachment of soldiers, Pike voyaged up the Mississippi River.   Besides parties of Indians, he came across British traders, some of whom had stations south of the falls of St. Anthony.   Pike established his winter-quarters north of that point. When the snow and ice had become hard enough for travelling he set out with a small party to travel overland to the head-waters of the great river.   His journey proved to be full of hardship and peril; had it not been for the assistance of the employees of the British Northwest Company and other British traders disaster might well have put an end to the expedition.   As it was, he could not dispossess the

[1] *Original Journals of Lewis and Clark Expedition* (Thwaites's ed.), II., 79.
[2] Coues, *Expeditions of Zebulon Montgomery Pike*, I., 1.

intruders of their belongings and drive them over
the border into their own territory. On the other
hand, he had to accept their hospitality and supplies. It is interesting to note, however, that these
traders were within territory which was clearly outside of British dominions. With the ground and
the lake and river surfaces covered with snow and
ice, it was impossible for the explorers to ascertain accurately the exact source of the Mississippi.
Pike therefore made a mistake as to the head-stream,
which was not at all to be wondered at, considering
the low-lying character of the region around the
headwaters of the Mississippi, the Red River, and
the Lake of the Woods. Pike's return to St. Louis
was easily accomplished. He arrived at headquarters at St. Louis in April, 1806, and in the
following August, before the return of Lewis and
Clark, was off again; this time to the exploration of
the Arkansas and the country to the south of the
Missouri.

The genesis of the western exploration of Pike[1] is
not clear. He made it in pursuance of orders from
General Wilkinson, but whether this action of Wilkinson was the result of orders from Washington
is not known. It seems unlikely that Wilkinson
would have sent a detachment of his small army
into a region which was in dispute between the
United States and Spain without the authorization

[1] This exploration is described in Coues, *Expeditions of Zebulon Montgomery Pike*, II.

of those who were responsible for the management
of the international relations of the country; but
Wilkinson had great facility in covering his purposes, and, indeed, his acts. It seems improbable
that Pike would have pursued the route that he
followed without express orders from his commanding officer. At all events, whatever the facts
as to the origin and purposes of the expedition may
have been, the enterprise itself proved to be more
dangerous than either of the northern expeditions.
Pike's route led him into the country occupied by
the nomadic tribes of the southern plains. With
the grim determination to do his duty or die in the
attempt which marked his career—even to its tragic
ending at York—Pike faced tremendous odds; his
firmness overawed even a returning unsuccessful war-
party of Pawnees. Following the general course of
the Arkansas, at first on the river itself and later
on horseback, at length Pike and his soldiers reached
the site of the modern town of Pueblo, in Colorado.
Leaving most of his men in camp at that point, Pike
essayed the closer examination of the mountain mass
which still commemorates his constancy and courage.

The history of the expedition from this point is
more difficult to follow. It may be that Pike was
merely seeking the head-waters of the Arkansas and
lost his way. The more probable opinion, in the
case of an experienced explorer like Zebulon Pike,
is that he had orders to penetrate to the Rio Grande
and reconnoitre the Spanish positions there. Con-

sidering the claims of the United States to the country east and north of that river, there was no reason why an expedition should not be sent there provided the government was prepared to go to war with Spain, which had such rights as possession could give. At all events, Pike, in search of either the Arkansas or the Rio Grande, ventured too far into the mountains, considering the season of the year, or perhaps lost his way. Starvation and frost-bites, in some cases fatal, were the result. At length Pike, with a few companions, encamped near the Spanish settlements on the Rio Grande. He was succored by the Spanish authorities, conducted in a roundabout way through northern Mexico and Texas, and released at the frontier.

In this peregrination he was accompanied by eight of his men; another party had descended the Arkansas from its upper waters. What became of the rest of the party cannot be definitely stated. Some of them died in the mountains; the rest either made their way homeward over the plains, were escorted through Texas by the Spaniards, or were taken to Mexico by their captors and there detained. Returning to civilization, Pike sat himself down and wrote out an account of his two expeditions, which is still one of the most interesting narratives of exploration in existence. It was published immediately, and gave to Pike an immediate fame, which he deserved, albeit somewhat to the disadvantage of Lewis and Clark. They had reached the mountains before Pike, had successfully crossed and recrossed them at the expense of great suffering, but without expense of human life or disaster. Nevertheless, when one thinks of the exploration of the Rocky Mountains the name of Zebulon Montgomery Pike comes first to mind.

In turning over in one's memory the story of these expeditions, one is impressed by the scantiness of the Indian population and by the general friendliness of the natives to the whites—although there were some exceptions to this general feeling of trustfulness. It is noteworthy, however, that the tribes in the far interior, like the Nez Percés, behaved with a generosity and degree of fidelity in sharp contrast to the qualities displayed by those tribes which had been long in contact with the white traders and trappers.

CHAPTER VIII

SLAVERY AND THE SLAVE-TRADE

(1801–1808)

THE decade covered by this volume falls within a period of comparative quietude in the conflict over slavery.[1] Nevertheless, it is not entirely devoid of interest, even from this point of view. The antislavery agitation which had its rise in the political theories and philanthropic tendencies of the revolutionary epoch had spent itself. Slavery was doomed in the north, where it was economically unprofitable; agitation could only hasten its demise. The fear of free blacks, even in communities where the sight of a man of color was unusual, met the abolitionist at every point. The dread of a free black population was the outcome of the feeling of dislike which white people felt for the social equality of the blacks which such a status seemed to imply, and to the belief that the free blacks committed crimes out of all proportion to their number. The white people of the north, furthermore, could not reconcile their thrifty minds to the idea of support-

[1] See Locke, *Anti-Slavery before 1808* (*Radcliffe Monographs*, No. 11.), chap. v.

ing the freedmen at the public charge when too old
to labor; there seemed something incongruous in
the idea of white men supporting black men except
when the latter had earned the right to consideration by long service in the relation of slave to
master.

Under these circumstances the utmost that the
reformers could accomplish, even in so strong an
antislavery state as Pennsylvania, resulted in a
proposition to tax the free blacks to provide funds
for purchasing their congeners in slavery.[1] On the
other hand, however, the friends of the negro were
able to secure the passage of laws[2] forbidding northern masters to relieve themselves of their burdens
by shipping their slaves to the markets of the south.
In the south the antislavery agitation had dwindled
for a very different reason: negro labor had become
profitable. The invention of the cotton-gin made
the cultivation of the cotton-plant profitable in the
older slave states of the southeast; the acquisition of
Louisiana opened to southerners a region to which
slave labor was peculiarly adapted—it provided a
market for any possible surplus of slaves in Virginia,
North Carolina, and Kentucky. The demand for
negro slaves increased out of all proportion to the
supply.

The southerners especially dreaded the presence

---

[1] Locke, *Anti-Slavery before 1808* (*Radcliffe Monographs*, No.
11), 127.
[2] See, for example, Paterson, *Laws of New Jersey*, 310.

of free blacks in their midst.   They had the terrify-
ing spectacle of Toussaint L'Ouverture and his black
companions always before their eyes.   It is true that
the negro race had produced but one black Napoleon in centuries, but the southerners saw many
such another in the free blacks around them.   They
believed that the safety of their wives and children
was menaced by the presence of any considerable
number of free blacks in their neighborhood—if they
should become too numerous and could not be disposed of peaceably they must be sold into slavery or
killed.[1]   One result of the general panic over the
influence of Santo Domingan negroes in stirring up
rebellion was the passage of an act of Congress in
aid of state laws prohibiting the slave-trade.   This
law provided for the forfeiture of the ship and punishment of the captain bringing any person of color,
slave or free, into any state which prohibited such
importation or immigration.[2]

The year (1803) that saw the passage of the act
described in the preceding paragraph also saw the
repeal by South Carolina of the law of that state for
the prohibition of slaves into that state.   South
Carolina now opened its ports undisguisedly to a
new incoming tide of negro slaves.   It is probably

[1] This statement is based on an inference from the speech of
Representative Early of Georgia, in the House, in the debate of
1807.

[2] *Laws of the United States*, VI., 212 (Acts of 2 Sess. of 7 Cong.,
chap. x.); *Statutes at Large*, II., 205.   On legislation prior to
1801, see Bassett, *Federalist System* (*Am. Nation*, XI.), chap. xii.

true that the prohibitory laws of the southern states could not be enforced, owing to the great demand for negro labor in that section, and it is doubtless correct as a matter of theory that, when a law cannot be enforced because it is contrary to public opinion, it would better be withdrawn. Nevertheless, it is certain that pecuniary advantage was at the bottom of the action of South Carolina. Whatever the reason, the fact aroused great attention in Congress and the country.

In those days Pennsylvania was the home of the most determined and aggressive abolitionists. It happened, therefore, that in January, 1804, a few weeks after the repeal of the South Carolina law, Representative Bard, of Pennsylvania, moved in the House that a tax of ten dollars per head should be laid on all negroes imported into the United States.[1] The Constitution forbade the prohibition of the slave-trade before 1808, and limited the amount that could be levied by way of head-money at ten dollars. Considering that the value of a negro slave was understood to average four hundred dollars, this tax cannot be regarded as a high one. The proposition, however, aroused debate. Bard stated that the action of South Carolina opened the floodgates of incalculable miseries to the country. The South Carolina congressmen deprecated the action of their state, but opposed vigorously this attempt to limit a state's constitutional action by federal law. They fur-

[1] *Annals of Cong.*, 8 Cong., 1 Sess., 820.

bished up all the old arguments: the levying of any tax would give a federal sanction to the trade; the proposed tax would be inequitable, because it would be levied on only one state and on only one industry, agriculture; it was inadvisable because the law would render it more difficult to prohibit the trade in 1808. To these arguments of 1793[1] was now added the further assertion that the proposed action would look like an attempt to punish a state for exercising its rights. These arguments appealed to the House, and the matter, after prolonged debate, was dropped.[2]

The debates of 1803 on Bard's resolution, and of 1804 on the limitation of slave importations into the Louisiana purchase, stirred the reformers to renewed vigor. Their efforts now took the shape of petitions for a constitutional amendment giving Congress power to deal with the slave-trade at once. The legislatures of North Carolina, Massachusetts, Vermont, New Hampshire, and Maryland passed resolutions on the subject, and a joint resolution was introduced into the national House of Representatives to overthrow one of the compromises which had made the adoption of the Constitution possible; but nothing came of the attempt   In 1805, and again in 1806, the question of taxation came up in Congress.[3] The proposition in its final form was to

---

[1] See Bassett, *Federalist System* (*Am. Nation*, XI.), chap. xii.
[2] *Annals of Cong.*, 8 Cong., 1 Sess., 991 et seq.
[3] See Locke, *Anti-Slavery before 1808* (*Radcliffe Monographs*, No. 11), 145.

lay a tax of ten dollars per head on all persons of
color, slave and free, brought in. Other matters
were pressing for attention, in two years' time the
whole trade could be prohibited; why, then, waste
time and energy in imposing a tax which, if it were
laid at all, would provide an argument against the
total abolition of the trade?

Thomas Jefferson had been an opposer of the
slave-trade since his entrance into public life. In
1774 he had included among the grievances against
the English government the disallowance of Virginia
bills for regulating and prohibiting the importation
of slaves into the province. In the Declaration of
Independence he had returned to the charge, and
in the original draft of that great instrument
had stigmatized the slave-trade as "piratical warfare" and a cruel war against human nature; but
these savage arraignments of the British government and of many of his fellow-colonists had been
excised from the final form of the instrument by
vote of Congress. Jefferson, Washington, Patrick
Henry, and John Randolph of Roanoke were opposed to slavery in theory; they saw, however, that
the circumstances of the case were against immediate emancipation. Whether it could ever be
brought about, and in what manner, they could not
foretell. Here, at last, was an opportunity to do
something to limit the further importation of negroes
into the United States. In his annual message[1] of

[1] Richardson, *Messages and Papers*, I., 408.

December, 1806, Jefferson called the attention of Congress to the approach of the period at which the federal government might prohibit "those violations of human rights which have been so long continued on the unoffending inhabitants of Africa, and which the morality, the reputation, and the best interests of our country have long been eager to proscribe." In answer, Senator Bradley of Vermont introduced a bill into the Senate for the total prohibition of the traffic from and after January 1, 1808. In the House the matter was referred to a committee, of which Peter Early of Georgia was chairman, and on which southerners were in a majority. Although the suggestion of the president was acted on with so great promptness, it turned out to be a matter of great difficulty and one requiring much time to pass a bill on which a majority could agree.[1]

Any measure to be effective necessarily provided for the limitation or regulation of the coastwise carrying of slaves from one state of the Union to another. It was proposed to prohibit it entirely, or, at least, to forbid the coasting trade to vessels below forty tons' burden. It was in this part of the debate that John Randolph intervened. He was opposed to slavery, and in 1821 provided by

[1] See *Annals of Cong.*, 9 Cong., 2 Sess., passim. The debates are summarized in Locke, *Anti-Slavery before 1808* (*Radcliffe Monographs*, No. 11), 150–155, and Du Bois, *Suppression of the Slave-Trade* (*Harvard Historical Studies*, No. 1.), chap. viii.

will for the emancipation of his slaves at his death. As a leader of the Virginia aristocracy and as a statesman of the Virginia school, he had other views: he saw in this proposition an attack on the political rights of Virginia as a state and on slave-holders as a class. It was an infringement on the rights of "property." It restricted the slave-owner in the exercise of rights which were guaranteed by the constitution. He prophesied that if ever the Union should split asunder the line of cleavage would be between the slave and free states and not between the east and the west. Slavery was property, the rights of property were in danger, the constitutional rights of southerners were threatened. These statements carry the historical student forward to the Missouri Compromise and the days of 1850. Randolph was eccentric, he was ahead of his time, but he had the foresight of the true prophet.[1] To Randolph's statements Early of Georgia made an important contribution when he declared that "a large majority of the people in the southern states do not consider slavery as a crime."[2] Pecuniary interest and personal convenience had brought a majority of the people in the south to regard the presence of the slaves as a benefit. The alignment of parties curiously bore out Randolph's prediction. The Pennsylvania Democrats joined the Massachusetts Federalists to carry out the policy of the Vir-

---

[1] Annals of Cong., 9 Cong., 2 Sess., 626, 636.
[2] Ibid., 9 Cong., 2 Sess., 238.

ginian president in the teeth of the opposition of his supporters in southern states.

The House bill, as it came from the committee, provided that persons of color illegally imported into the United States should be forfeited and sold for life for the benefit of the United States. Sloan, of New Jersey, at once moved as an amendment that the illegally imported and forfeited slaves should immediately be set free. The antislavery men could not accept the idea that the United States could acquire a title to human beings. The slaves could not be taken back to Africa, for they were usually negroes from the interior who had been secured by the coast tribes by purchase or by war and sold to the white traders. To land them on the coast of Africa would be to return them to a worse form of slavery than that which prevailed in America. To indenture them for a term of years in a free state seemed a hopeful solution to many. In the end a compromise course was adopted by which the captured slaves were turned over to the authorities of the state where the ship was condemned, to be disposed of according to state law.

The greatest excitement, however, was aroused over the question of what should be done with the captured slaver. Should he be put to death or sentenced to fine and imprisonment? On the one hand it was argued that the slave-trader was worse than the murderer, because he added kidnapping to murder. On the other hand, it was argued that

to punish the crime too severely would defeat the
ends of justice, because no one would inform against
a trader if his capture meant death.   A milder penalty would be more efficacious in a community which
did not recognize slavery as morally wrong.   It was
not the southerners alone who took this position: a
Rhode Island member declared "that a man ought
not to be hung for only stealing a negro."   In the
end, after prolonged, acrimonious, and imperfectly
reported debates, the act[1] was passed prohibiting the
importation of slaves after January 1, 1808, on penalty of forfeiture of ship and cargo, a fine of from
one thousand to ten thousand dollars, and imprisonment of from five to ten years.   The coasting trade
was limited to vessels of forty tons and over, and the
slaves were to be registered.   This provision of the
law was so distasteful to John Randolph of Roanoke
that he secured permission to bring in a supplementary bill, but no action except to refer it was taken
before Congress came to an end.   Randolph also declared that the Virginia delegation would wait on the
president and protest against his signing the bill, but
nothing came of that.   Notwithstanding Randolph's
vigorous denunc ation of the act as passed, it can
hardly be regarded as a victory for the antislavery interests.   The captured Africans were to be retained
in the position of slavery, and the penalty proved to
be entirely inadequate.   The abolition of the Brit-

[1] *Laws of the United States*, VIII., 262; Acts of 9 Cong., 2 Sess.,
chap. xxii.; *U. S. Statutes at Large*, II., 426.

ish slave-trade by act of Parliament, at nearly the same time, gave added efficacy to the American act. For half a century there were slaves imported into the United States, but their numbers were but as driblets in comparison to what they would have been had it not been for the condemnation contained in the act of 1807 and the supplementary acts which were passed from time to time.[1]

[1] For the progress of slavery and antislavery after 1808, see Turner, *New West*, chap. xi.; Hart, *Slavery and Abolition*, passim (*Am. Nation*, XIV., XVI.).

CHAPTER IX

THE CHASE IMPEACHMENT

(1804–1805)

THE purchase of Louisiana completed the temporary ruin of the Federalist party; Jefferson's triumphant re-election, in 1804, was an assured fact. Nevertheless, it seemed to be desirable to change the language of the Constitution with a view to prevent any more disputed elections like that which had nearly resulted in making Aaron Burr chiefmagistrate. This proved to be, however, by no means the easy task which one would have expected. In the first place, the reform proposed consisted in requiring the presidential electors to vote specifically for president and vice-president.[1] This would prevent any misunderstanding as to which person was intended for the higher office. At the same time, however, it would work injury to the smaller states, for the candidate for the second office would certainly be some person who was supposed to be popular in a politically doubtful large state. Moreover, many northern members of Congress felt that if any change in the Constitution were made, the

[1] *Annals of Cong.*, 8 Cong., 1 Sess., 268.

first thing to be attacked should be the "federal ratio" which gave an undue amount of power to the south. The result of these considerations was that the proposed amendment was voted down when it first made its appearance in Congress. 'A second time it had better fortune, and was finally passed just in time to serve as the rule in the election of 1804.

Jefferson once wrote that "Pennsylvania seems to have in its bowels a good deal of volcanic matter, and some explosion may be expected."[1] This sentence was penned in August, 1804; but the volcano had already labored more than once. Perhaps nothing in the Constitution of the United States is more extraordinary than the failure of that instrument to provide any means for getting rid of the judges of the federal courts except by the process of impeachment. In England, in Massachusetts, and in Pennsylvania, judges could be removed by the executive upon address by both branches of the legislative body. In none of these cases was it necessary to allege or to prove any criminal act on the part of the judge. In colonial days the tenure of the judicial office had been of the weakest. In the royal provinces, the judges had been appointed by the crown and had been removable at pleasure. In the charter colonies, the judges had been appointed by the legislature, and their tenure of office was generally for one year. The precarious-

[1] Jefferson, *Writings* (Ford's ed.), VIII., 318.

ness of judicial office in the royal provinces had more than once led to attempts on the part of the colonists to secure greater permanency, because a permanent judiciary would afford them protection against the royal authorities. All attempts of this kind, however, had been defeated by the negative voice of the government in England. Possibly the permanence of judicial tenure which is found in the Constitution of the United States may be regarded in some sort as the result of this pre-revolutionary contest. At all events, the Constitution provided no means to secure the removal of a judge of the supreme court of the United States, save impeachment. Judges of inferior United States courts might be "legislated out of office" by the destruction of the courts in which they sat; but the supreme court existed by virtue of the Constitution itself, and could not be destroyed by an act of Congress. The judges of the supreme court, therefore, seemed to have an impregnable hold upon the bench.

The Republicans of Pennsylvania pointed out that the way to deal with this matter was to use the process of impeachment to get rid of obnoxious judges against whom nothing criminal could be proved. In that state, President Judge Addison, of one of the five courts of common pleas, was impeached (1) for refusing to permit a colleague to make a political address to the grand jury, and (2) for being insolent towards his Democratic colleagues in some remarks which he himself had addressed to the grand jurors. The Pennsylvania senate voted him guilty, removed him from office, and adjudged him incapable of sitting as a judge in any Pennsylvania court.[1] The Pennsylvania legislature then pushed on the impeachment of three of the four judges of the state supreme court (1804). In this attempt they did not have the success which had attended the earlier efforts against Judge Addison. The three judges who were marked out for slaughter were Federalists, but the fourth, Judge Hugh A. Breckenridge, a Republican, promptly wrote to the legislature asking to be impeached with his brethren. The whole legal profession caught the alarm. Alexander J. Dallas, Jefferson's district attorney in Pennsylvania, had been willing to prosecute Addison, but he now not only refused to lead the prosecution against the supreme court judges, but actually led the defence. Not a Pennsylvania lawyer of reputation could be found to do the work, and Cæsar A. Rodney, of Delaware, had to be summoned from Congress to stand against Dallas and those who labored with him. In the end, the state senate declined, 13 to 11, to vote the judges guilty.[2]

The attack on the federal judges began with the impeachment of Judge Pickering of the New Hampshire district court. This judge, by his habits of intoxication, had rendered himself partly insane,

---

[1] *Trial of Alexander Addison, Esq., on an Impeachment before the Senate of Pennsylvania* (1803).

[2] *Trial of the Pennsylvania Judges on an Impeachment* (1805).

or perhaps insane tendencies had impelled him to
overindulgence in strong drink.[1] Whichever was
the case, it was quite evident that Judge Pickering
was not a fit person to sit in any court, and yet there
was no way to secure his removal except by the
process of impeachment. The president called the
attention of the House to the matter in a brief
message which he transmitted to the House of
Representatives, because the Constitution had confided to that body the power to institute proceedings
for redress. The trial began before the Senate,
sitting as a court of impeachment on March 2, 1804.
Judge Pickering was not present, but a petition
came from his son asking for a postponement of
the trial so that he might offer evidence as to the insanity of his father during the last two years, when
the acts alleged against him had been committed;
and Robert Goodloe Harper asked to be allowed
to appear on behalf of the petitioner. After a long
debate the Senate admitted Harper, and the judge's
insanity was made clear. After further debate the
Senate voted that Judge Pickering was guilty as
charged and ought to be removed from office. This
was surely a most extraordinary conclusion to reach,
but it was the only way in which an insane judge
could be removed from the bench to make room for
a man who was possessed of his senses.

After Judge Pickering's impeachment had been

[1] *Message enclosing Documents relating to John Pickering, District Judge of New Hampshire* (1803).

decided on by the House, but before the case was tried by the Senate, an old revolutionary hero, Samuel Chase of Maryland, one of the justices of the supreme court of the United States, stated his opinions in regard to the democratizing tendencies of the dominant party. May 2, 1803, he addressed the grand jury at Baltimore, declaring that the introduction of universal suffrage would destroy personal liberty and would sink the republican Constitution into a mobocracy, which was the worst of all possible governments.[1] He concluded with the statement that the modern doctrines "that all men in a state of society are entitled to enjoy equal liberty and equal rights, have brought this mighty mischief upon us; and I fear that it will rapidly progress until peace and order, freedom and property, shall be destroyed." When Jefferson read this effusion, he sat down and wrote to Joseph Nicholson, who was the chairman of the committee of managers of the Pickering impeachment, asking him whether this seditious and official attack on the principles of the Constitution should go unpunished? For myself, said Jefferson, "It is better that I should not interfere."[2]

This was a regular Jeffersonian way of doing things. Precisely what action should be taken was undoubtedly not clear to him. Whether, indeed, any action at all should be had was a matter for

[1] *Answer and Pleas of Samuel Chase*, 65.
[2] Jefferson, *Works* (Congress. ed.), IV., 486.

consideration. Whether Jefferson ever went beyond giving this hint cannot be definitely stated. It certainly is not known that he ever approved the form which the impeachment took or the way in which it was conducted. At the moment, he was in a state of great irritation against the supreme court, for barely eight weeks had elapsed since John Marshall had given his extraordinary decision in the case of Marbury vs. Madison.

In a bill signed by President Adams about a week before his exit from office, provision had been made for the appointment of justices of the peace for the District of Columbia to hold office for five years. Adams nominated several persons to these offices, and the appointments were confirmed by the Senate at one of its last meetings. The commissions were found on Marshall's desk regularly filled out and signed by the president and attested by John Marshall, who, in the last weeks of Adams's administration, enacted the dual rôles of chief-justice of the supreme court and secretary of state. Levi Lincoln filled this latter office in the early days of Jefferson's government, until Madison could finish private business and assume the duties of the office. Lincoln did not deliver the commissions of those "midnight judges," as Jefferson stigmatized them, nor did Madison after him. William Marbury, one of the disappointed place - seekers, moved in the supreme court for a writ of mandamus to compel

Madison to deliver the withheld commission.[1] Congress, by postponing[2] the session of the supreme court for fifteen months, put off the decision, and also, it would be supposed, gave Marshall time to think the matter over carefully. When it did come, however, his opinion was phrased in such a manner that this is the one decision in Marshall's judicial career which still gives pain to all but his blindest admirers.

The chief-justice, in delivering the opinion of the court, declared, first, that Marbury had a right to the commission; second, that the refusal of the commission was a plain violation of that right for which the laws of the United States afforded Marbury a remedy. As to the remedy, however, Marshall was equally clear that the authority given to the supreme court in the law of 1789, establishing the judicial courts of the United States, to issue writs of mandamus to public officers, appears not to be warranted by the Constitution, on the ground that the supreme court has no original jurisdiction in such cases. He then proceeded at great length and in clearest language to set forth his opinion that when a law is at variance with the Constitution the court must cling to the Constitution and refuse to obey an act of Congress. He concluded with, "The rule must be discharged."

[1] 1 Curtis, 368.
[2] This was done at the time of the repeal of the Judiciary Act; see above, p. 27.

No practice of the judicial branch of the government has been of more dangerous consequence than the habit of the justices of the supreme court of discussing questions upon which the decision of the court does not rest. Moreover, in this case the chief-justice was, in a manner, sitting on the validity of his own act when secretary of state in attesting commissions which were issued in defiance of what the head of the executive branch regarded as decency and good politics. Marshall stated that the court had no jurisdiction in the case before it, and then, with ill-concealed joy, went on to lay down the doctrine that the supreme court is not bound by acts of Congress or by the interpretation of its powers by the executive. Marshall's opinion was displeasing to southerners, even to southern Federalists. We find, for instance, John Steele, a Carolinian who remained faithful to the Hamiltonian ideal, writing to Macon[1] in condemnation of what he termed "the fashionable doctrine" that the courts might pronounce acts of Congress unconstitutional. If Madison had done wrong in withholding Marbury's commission, he could be punished by process of impeachment. Macon, curiously enough, was disposed to give more authority to the judicial branch. He acknowledged its supremacy, but thought that the judges would be slow to exercise their power of annulling laws, owing to their accountability to Congress. Many persons, at the time,

[1] Dodd, *Nathaniel Macon*, 184.

doubtless expected that when the Chase impeachment had been brought to a triumphant conclusion the Federalist chief-justice would be impeached for misbehavior in going so far afield from the business before him. But the Chase impeachment, in place of being brought to a triumphant conclusion, came to such a lame ending that the Federalist judges of the supreme court were firmly fixed in their seats.[1]

The one man in the House of Representatives who might have successfully prosecuted this trial was Joseph Nicholson of Maryland. Unfortunately, he was the man who was likely to profit by Chase's downfall, for he would certainly be appointed to take his place on the supreme bench. Under these circumstances the conduct of the impeachment fell mainly to John Randolph of Roanoke, and he made a sad business of it. Instead of impeaching Chase for delivering a political harangue while sitting on the bench, the managers preferred no less than eight charges. Of these, two had to do with Chase's conduct in the trial of Fries and Callender, and the fifth and sixth threatened the integrity of the federal judicial system. The result was that the members of the supreme court, with the chief-justice at their head, rallied to the defence of their threatened prerogatives, and were joined by a large part of the legal fraternity of the United States, especially in the north. Chase found no difficulty

[1] See *Trial of Judge Chase on an Impeachment* (1805).

in securing the services of able and eminent lawyers.
On the other hand, the managers on the part of the
House, with the exception of Nicholson, were none of
them great lawyers, and, so far as they were lawyers
at all, must have been conscious that they were
fighting against the interest and prerogatives of
their class. Under these circumstances, the managers should have striven with the utmost vigor to
lay down the theory that the impeachment process
was in no sense like an indictment for crime, and
was, as a matter of fact, the only way by which a
meddlesome judge could be ejected from the bench.
Surely there is something absurd in the general
contention that a federal judge, like Samuel Chase,
should hold office for life and be at full liberty to
criticise in the most insolent way the agents to
whom the people have intrusted the management
of their affairs. Nevertheless, that tremendous respect for "the law," which is at once the strength
•and the greatest weakness of the American character, enabled the supreme court and the legal
fraternity to secure the acquittal of Chase on the
general ground that a man could not be impeached
for that which was not indictable. Twenty-three
votes were needed to secure conviction. On only
one charge did as many as nineteen senators vote
Chase guilty. That charge was the eighth, having to
do with his political harangue, and on that it seems
not unlikely Chase might have been convicted and
removed from office had not prejudices and resent-

ments been aroused by combining with this so many other matters. The result of the failure of the impeachment was to place John Marshall firmly in power and to wreck the political future of John Randolph of Roanoke.

Returning to the House of Representatives, Randolph and Nicholson moved the adoption of two amendments to the Constitution. Randolph's amendment provided for the removal of the judges of the supreme court of the United States and of all other federal courts by the president on the joint address of both Houses of Congress. This idea in itself had long experience to justify it and might well have been adopted. Coming from Randolph, at the precise moment that it did, it was only an example of the puerile petulance of his disordered mind. Nicholson, for his part, proposed that the legislature of any state might, whenever it saw fit, recall one or both of its senators and appoint one or more senators to fill their places. This arrangement in itself was perfectly logical from the state-rights point of view; but at the moment it marked only Nicholson's wrath with the Republican senators. Both propositions were referred to the next Congress, and nothing more was heard of either of them.[1]

Apart from the constitutional and political results of this trial, the most interesting point is the

---

[1] Ames, *Proposed Amendments to the Constitution* (Am. Hist. Assoc., *Annual Report*, 1896, vol. II.), 64.

theatrical setting which was given to it by its presiding officer, and the character and career of that presiding officer himself—or perhaps it would be better to say the lack of character of that remarkable personage and the sudden eclipse of his political career. In those days every one was affected by the accounts of the monstrously unfair trial of Warren Hastings, and by the reputation which Edmund Burke so unjustly secured from his eloquent harangues on that occasion. John Randolph of Roanoke seems to have been attracted to the Chase affair largely in the expectation that he, too, by vituperation, might secure immortality. In the interval between the vote of the House to impeach Chase and the actual trial before the Senate, Aaron Burr met Alexander Hamilton on the duelling - ground at Weehawken and killed him. For a time he was a fugitive in the south, but returned to Washington in time to preside at the trial. It seemed to be pretty certain that a good deal depended on the part which Burr should feel inclined to play. Jefferson recognized this, and, although he cannot have approved of the way in which the Chase affair was managed, he seems to have done his best to endeavor to placate the vice-president. Offices were given to his wife's relatives and connections. His friend General Wilkinson was made governor of Louisiana territory, although by so doing Jefferson united in one hand civil and military power. Jefferson even invited Burr to dinner, and Madison and Gallatin renewed their old friendships with him, and Republican senators petitioned the governor of New Jersey to defeat his indictment for murder. Indeed, everything was done to bring him to the side of the administration.

These blandishments of Jefferson and his ministers seem only to have encouraged the vice-president to cause the Senate chamber to be fitted up with a splendor which, had the Federalists been responsible, would have been visited with anathema by Jefferson and the *Aurora*. On the right and the left of the vice-president's chair, two rows of benches covered with crimson cloth were arranged for the senators, galleries covered with green cloth were set apart for the women, distinguished guests, and members of the House of Representatives, while two boxes or pens, covered with blue cloth, were reserved for the managers of the impeachment and for the accused and his counsel.[1]

In the midst of these impeachment trials, Jefferson was re-elected president. For the first time in the history of the United States a candidate for that office was nominated by a congressional caucus of senators and representatives. Nominating conventions had been held before this in some of the states. The practice was now extended to national affairs. The Federalists held no convention, but agreed among themselves to vote for Charles C. Pinckney. It really made slight difference whether

[1] Adams, *United States*, II., 226, 227.

they had a candidate or not. Jefferson received 162
electoral votes to 14 cast for Pinckney.   Even Massachusetts voted for Jefferson.   Connecticut alone
remained "solid" for the Federalists.[1]

[1] Stanwood, *Hist. of the Presidency*, 84.

CHAPTER X

JOHN RANDOLPH AND THE YAZOO MEN

(1801–1813)

IN 1829, John Randolph of Roanoke accepted an appointment as special minister to Russia. He remained ten days at his post, passed the greater part of a year in England, returned home to the United States, drew $21,407 from the national treasury, and paid off a debt with which his estate had been saddled since his earliest years. Says Henry Adams: "This act of Roman virtue, worthy of the satire of Juvenal, still stands as the most flagrant bit of diplomatic jobbery in the annals of the United States government."[1] Curiously enough, in 1804 John Randolph looked upon himself as an incorruptible man, while language failed even him to describe the sins of the old Yazoo speculators. "You are a Yazoo man, Mr. Watkins,"[2] said Randolph to a political opponent, pointing at him with his long finger, and Captain Watkins had not the prescience to retort upon him: "One day you will be the biggest diplomatic jobber in American annals."

[1] Adams, *John Randolph* (*Am. Statesmen Series*), 296.
[2] *Ibid.*, 260.

The Yazoo business, in its various ramifications, is probably the most complicated historical problem[1] in the annals of the United States. The main elements of the story, however, can be stated somewhat roughly, if one remembers that probably every statement one might make on the subject would bear qualification. The western boundary of Georgia for a long time was disputed between Georgia, South Carolina, and the United States. The original Georgia charter of 1732 carved out a bit of territory from South Carolina and formed it into the government of Georgia, which for a number of years was under the rule of a set of philanthropists who were known collectively as the Georgia Trustees.[2] By this grant Georgia extended westward directly south of the southern boundary of the main portion of South Carolina. South of Georgia lay another portion of South Carolina, which had no white inhabitants and served as a species of "neutral ground" between the English and the Spanish colonies. In 1763 the king of Great Britain became possessed of all of North America east of the Mississippi River and east of the island of Orleans. In parcelling out this tract, for purposes of administration, he limited East Florida on the north by the St. Mary's River, and added to Georgia the territory between that river and Georgia's original southern boundary; in other words, the king

[1] For a local view, see E. J. Harden, *George M. Troup*, passim.
[2] Cf. Greene, *Provincial America* (*Am. Nation*, VI.), chap. xv.

gave another slice of South Carolina to Georgia. In this same proclamation the king reserved for the Indians, subject to future changes, territory west and northwest of the heads of rivers which emptied into the Atlantic Ocean.[1] As South Carolina and Georgia, as well as the Floridas, were all royal provinces at this time, the king's right to make whatever disposition he saw fit of this territory would seem to be indisputable. At the time of the Revolution, however, both Georgia and South Carolina claimed the territory south of Georgia's southern charter boundary and between the Mississippi River and the "Proclamation Line." When the treaty of peace came, the United States in Congress assembled also put forward a claim to a large part of this land, on the ground that it, or most of it, at all events, had been governed by the British, as a part of West Florida.[2]

Meantime, in 1785, the legislature of Georgia formed the strip immediately east of the Mississippi River into Bourbon County. In 1789 the legislature of the same state sold lands in this region to citizens of Virginia and of the Carolinas, under the guise of the Virginia Yazoo Company, the South Carolina Yazoo Company, and the Tennessee Company. These enterprising land-jobbers proposed

[1] Cf. Howard, *Preliminaries of the Revolution* (*Am. Nation*, VIII.), chap. xiii., and maps at pp. 4, 298.
[2] Cf. McLaughlin, *Confederation and Constitution* (*Am. Nation*, X.), chap. vi.

to pay for these lands with Georgia paper money, although they agreed not to tender the most worthless Georgia bills, which were locally called "rattlesnake money." Georgia reccived some of the money, and then refused to receive more of the same kind as payment for the rest of the lands. The South Carolina Yazoo Company sued Georgia in the United States supreme court, but was left without any legal remedy by the adoption of the Eleventh Amendment, which was declared in force January 8, 1798.[1]

With a view still further to complicate matters, if possible, in 1794 the Georgia legislature sold the same land, or a part of it, to four other land companies. At this time, however, the governor interposed his veto, stating his objections to the act. The legislature promptly removed the objectionable features, and the law was then passed in 1795. It then appeared that the members of the Georgia legislature who had voted for the act had been bribed. The people of Georgia held a "convention" and made so great a noise that the Georgia legislature, in 1796, declared the act of 1795 to be null and void.[2] President Washington now intervened. Acting largely on his initiative, Congress some time later, in the administration of John Adams (1798), established the territory of Mississippi with a government like that of the northwest territory, without, however, the

---

[1] Haskins, *Yazoo Land Co.* (Am. Hist. Assoc., *Report*, 1891); cf. Bassett, *Federalist System* (*Am. Nation*, XI.), chap. v.
[2] E. J. Harden, *George M. Troup*, 14–19, 48–84.

clause forbidding the introduction of slavery, and made provision for a joint commission to settle the claims of Georgia and of the United States. Commissioners were duly appointed, but nothing had been accomplished when Jefferson became president. The business now fell into the hands of the commission, which was made up of Madison, Gallatin, Lincoln, and three Georgians — Senators Jackson and Baldwin and Governor Milledge.

The settlement which was reached was mainly the work of Gallatin—that is, so far as the details were concerned. It provided, in brief, (1) an extension of Georgia to the west to give her the present boundary; (2) the extinction of the Indian title to lands within her limits by the United States as soon as it could conveniently be done; (3) the payment of one million two hundred and fifty thousand dollars to the state from the net proceeds of the lands in the territory to which she abandoned her claims; (4) the admission of the ceded territory to the Union as a slave state whenever its inhabitants should number sixty thousand; and (5) the setting aside five million acres of land to satisfy the claims under the several acts of the Georgia legislature which have been described above. This last provision was made avowedly to promote the tranquillity of those persons who should hereafter inhabit within the new territory and state.

When a bill ratifying this arrangement came before the House of Representatives, late in January, 1803, John Randolph of Roanoke attacked the measure with a ferocity unusual even in him.[1] Randolph at this time was excessively jealous of his fellow-Virginian James Madison — or, possibly, hostile would better express the idea. The form in which the Georgia Yazoo business had been settled was in itself objectionable because the leading members of the cabinet were personally responsible for it; but that was due to a provision in the act of Congress providing for the appointment of the commission; with the drawing of this law Madison had had nothing to do. The administration was necessarily interested in pushing the bill because the prestige of Madison and of Gallatin demanded its passage. John Randolph was on terms of intimacy with Gallatin as he was with no other man, excepting only Joseph Nicholson. He persisted, however, in attributing this settlement which gave the proceeds of five million acres of land to the holders of the Yazoo land warrants to Madison and not to Gallatin. Randolph moved to exclude the claimants under the Georgia act of 1795 from any participation in this settlement. Later, in 1804, he substituted for this resolution other resolutions which affirmed the legality of the Georgia act of 1796, repealing the law of 1795, and forbade the appropriation of money for the settlement of the claims under the Georgia grants. At the moment

[1] Randolph's speech of March 29, 1806, gives a convenient summary of his side of the case.

he was at the height of his power, and by hard work succeeded in defeating action on the bill.

By this action of Randolph the Yazoo matter assumed a phase which promised to bring about an interesting constitutional contest. The administration wished to avoid all question of constitutional law in the proposed settlement, even at the price of giving the proceeds of five million acres of land to those who might or might not have a good title under the Georgia grants. While Randolph proposed that Congress should lend its authority to a declaration that a state could annul contracts which it had entered into, in another part of the capitol John Marshall and his Federalist colleagues in the supreme court were eagerly awaiting the opportunity to declare that under the constitution of the United States no state could pass any law impairing the obligation of contracts.

Meantime the New England Mississippi Company had most unfortunately secured the services of Gideon Granger of Connecticut, the postmaster-general, to look after their interests at Washington. The discussion of the Yazoo matter began anew in January, 1805, just before the beginning of the active part of the Chase trial. Randolph had been in Georgia at the time of the excitement over the Yazoo grant of 1795. The sight of Gideon Granger on the floor of the House of Representatives urging members to vote for the passage of the Yazoo bill aroused in him the most vivid recollections of those

scenes. In the debate which followed he surpassed all
previous efforts in the use of vituperative language.
Formerly his invective had been directed against
Federalists and Monarchists, whereas now it was
used to besmirch the leaders of his own party. "Pol-
lution," "abomination," "corruption" were the mild-
est words he used. He asked, "Are the heads of executive departments to be brought into this House
. . . to extort from us now what we refused at the
last session of Congress? . . . For one . . . I should dis-
dain to prate about the petty larcenies of our predecessors after having given my sanction to this
atrocious public robbery."

In the House of Representatives with Randolph
was an old dealer in invective, Matthew Lyon, once
of Vermont and now of Kentucky. In former days
he had spat in Roger Griswold's face. He now
represented Kentucky and voted on the same side
with Griswold against Randolph, the latter charg-
ing him with jobbery on the floor of the House.
Lyon in return thanked his Creator that he himself had the face of a man and not that of an ape
or a monkey[1]—which plainly referred to the curious physiognomy of John Randolph of Roanoke.
Madison, on his part, was defended by his brother-
in-law, Representative Jackson of Virginia, in a
speech which had probably been concocted in
large part by the secretary of state. Randolph
had referred to Gideon Granger as a speculator

[1] McLaughlin, *Matthew Lyon*, 456.

whose gigantic grasp extended from the shores of Lake Erie to the mouth of the Mobile River. Jackson now described his colleague from Roanoke as a person whose "influence" was equal to the rapacity of the speculator just described. The House voted by a majority of 63 to 58 to proceed with the bill, but Randolph somehow succeeded for the moment in postponing any further action on the measure.

The fiasco of the Chase impeachment seems to have decided Randolph to abandon the cordial relations which up to that time he had maintained with the administration. In the summer of 1805, Jefferson stated that he should not a second time be a candidate for re-election. The reason for his taking this action is not difficult to find. His first administration had been successful beyond all anticipation; it was the "harvest season of his life," as he himself termed it. The harvest had been almost too complete. In the beginning of his first administration, with a united party at his back, he faced a disunited opposition. Now the opposition, if so it might be termed, was so feeble as to be of little moment, whether united or not; but success had brought disunion to Jefferson's own supporters. In Pennsylvania and in New York the Democrats were hopelessly divided; they were attacking one another with even more venom and vigor than they had attacked the once hated Federalists; the word "once" is here used advisedly, because the more aristocratic wing of the Republican party in the north every now and then dabbled with the Federalists. Jefferson tried to stand impartially between these factions. In New York this was a matter of no great difficulty, but in Pennsylvania it was impossible to keep on good terms with Duane and at the same time to give that support to the measures of Albert Gallatin which the secretary of the treasury required at the hands of his chief and friend.

South of Mason and Dixon's line, Jefferson's supporters were also divided into two factions. The revolution of 1800 had been fought by Jefferson and his southern friends on the grounds of high moral political philosophy. Power had since sapped the vigor of this morality. Many of the southerners were as eager for office as any Pennsylvania Democrat. Many of them were in alliance with the Yazoo men of the north; many of them, indeed, were themselves original Yazoo men. Within the ranks of Jefferson's supporters, therefore, there was fast developing a "split" in which the "old Republicans" of the south, with John Randolph of Roanoke at their head, were finding themselves in a hopeless minority when compared with the northern Democrats and the mass of the party in the south. Randolph seems intuitively to have realized what was going on; perhaps Jefferson also realized it, but was not so conscious of the lapse from high moral philosophy which was coming over the mass of the dominant party. He seems to have felt, at all events, that his active work was done, and that his refusal of a re-election in 1808 would be entirely justifiable (January, 1805).[1]

In October, 1805, Randolph[2] wrote to Gallatin— for he still maintained cordial relations with him— that he regretted exceedingly Jefferson's resolution to retire and the premature annunciation of that determination, partly on account of the intrigues which it will set on foot. "If I were sure," added Randolph, "that Monroe would succeed him, my regret would be very much diminished." What Randolph feared, but could hardly mention in a letter to the secretary of the treasury, was the fact that Madison was intended by Mr. Jefferson to be his successor, although perhaps no formal announcement of that decision had been made. Randolph distrusted Madison—regarded him as a Yazoo man, and as hopelessly weak. Himself, Randolph regarded as an "old Republican," and there was a good deal of truth in this idea; for, most of the time, he was faithful to the "principles of 1798."[3] He communicated his prejudices to Macon and a few other faithful personal friends. They began to act independently, and came to be known as the "Quids."

For three years the contest raged between Madison, with the administration behind him, on the one

[1] Jefferson, *Writings* (Ford's ed.), VIII., 338.
[2] Adams, *Randolph*, 161.
[3] See an interesting letter from Randolph to Monroe dated September 16, 1806, in Monroe, *Writings*, IV., 486 *n*.

side, and John Randolph on the other. In this
contest Madison and the administration won.
Randolph was deposed from the leadership of the
majority in the House of Representatives; his
friend Macon ceased to be speaker, and his other
friend, Nicholson, retired to the security of the
bench of the circuit court of Maryland. From
time to time Randolph and the few who remained
faithful to him were able to embarrass or to defeat
the administration. This was notably the case in
regard to the attempt to purchase West Florida
and the attempt, which finally was successful, to
confirm the Yazoo compromise by act of Congress.
The latter of these may well be now considered; the
former will be deferred to another chapter.

Year after year the Yazoo bill came up in Congress, and Randolph and his friends, with such help as
they could get, managed to defeat it. In 1810, however, the Yazoo men received great encouragement
from the decision given by Chief-Justice Marshall in
the case of Fletcher *vs.* Peck. This case arose over
the question of a title to land which rested ultimately on the Georgia act of 1795 which has been previously noted. In a detailed and luminous opinion,[1]
Marshall decided in favor of the title. In the course
of this decision he took up the point as to the
validity of the act of 1795, which was the result of
the operation of corrupt motives. Marshall thought

[1] Jefferson, however, referred to it as one of "the twistifica-
tions" of Marshall; see *Writings* (Ford's ed.), IX., 276.

that the fact of the corruption of the legislators could not in any way affect the title of an honest holder under the law, and doubted whether it was within the province of the judiciary to control the conduct of a bribed legislature. He did not say so, but the inference is not a violent one that the people of Georgia should have selected legislators who were not open to bribery. At all events, having chosen the legislature whose majority acted from impure motives, the people, whose representatives they were, were bound by their act. For these and other reasons, the title of an innocent holder under the act of 1795 in itself was good. Then Marshall took up the question of the validity of the Rescinding Act; he laid down the general principle that its validity might well be doubted were Georgia a single sovereign power. As a matter of fact, however, she was a member of the American Union, and in common with other states her legislature was limited in its power. Especially was this the case as to bills of attainder, *ex post facto* laws, and laws impairing the obligations of contracts. The Rescinding Act of 1796 was clearly an *ex post facto* law; it had some of the elements of an act of attainder in that it led to a confiscation of property, and it impaired the obligation of contracts, for a grant of land by legislative act was clearly a contract within the meaning of the Constitution.[1] The Eleventh Amendment had been adopted to preserve Georgia

[1] 6 Cranch, 87.

from the indignity of being sued by the Yazoo men;
and now the supreme court of the United States,
regardless of Georgia dignity, had decided that the
Yazoo land titles were good in law.

In the autumn of 1813, Randolph came before his
constituents for re-election. His seat was contested
by Jefferson's son-in-law, John W. Eppes. Randolph's opposition to the war with England at last
cost him the support of a faithful people. He was
defeated by Eppes, and the *Richmond Enquirer*,
joining in the pursuit of the fallen statesman, de-
nounced him as "a nuisance and a curse." Now,
at length, was the opportunity of the men of Yazoo.
In Randolph's absence, and even then with a majority of only eight votes, the House of Representatives provided for the payment of eight million
dollars[1] to the claimants under the Georgia land acts
(March, 1814). And thus ended one of the most
far-reaching contests in the political history of the
United States.

[1] *Laws of the United States*, X., 325 (Acts of 2 Sess., 13 Cong.,
chap. xxxix.); *U. S. Statutes at Large*, III., 116.

CHAPTER XI

THE END OF THE HARVEST SEASON
(1803–1805)

ON August 9, 1803, Thomas Jefferson wrote to his old friend and fellow-worker, the venerable John Dickinson, that Louisiana extended from the Iberville and the Mississippi on the east to the Mexicana, or the highlands east of it, on the west; then from the head of the Mexicana, along the highlands which include the waters of the Mississippi to the boundary of the English dominions, or perhaps to the Lake of the Woods. The United States also had "some pretensions" to extend the western territory of Louisiana to the Rio Grande del Norte, or Bravo; and even stronger pretensions to extend the eastern boundary of that purchase to the Rio Perdido.[1] Nearly a month after the date of this letter the Marquis of Casa Yrujo wrote to Madison, in the name of the Spanish government, protesting against the sale of Louisiana by France to the United States.[2] Yrujo's contention was that the United States had really bought stolen goods.

[1] Jefferson, *Writings* (Ford's ed.), VIII., 261.
[2] *Am. State Paps., Foreign*, II., 569.

Jefferson, in reply, ordered a strong body of soldiers to Natchez. Napoleon compelled the Spanish government to surrender Louisiana; but nothing could make the Frenchman admit that West Florida was within Louisiana, as it was retroceded by Spain to France. Even Laussat, the French commissioner, who handed Louisiana to Governor Claiborne, confidentially signified that the province extended westwardly to the Rio Bravo, otherwise called the Rio del Norte.[1] When the formal delivery was made, nothing was said on either side about West Florida.

The Marquis of Casa Yrujo had lived long in the United States, had married a daughter of that good Republican, Governor McKean of Pennsylvania, and was on terms of intimacy with Jefferson, Madison, and Gallatin. His long residence in America had somewhat softened his hidalgo temper and had also taught him the dangerous art of writing to the newspapers. On this occasion he was not content merely to write to the newspapers. Seething with indignation, he sought out a Federalist editor named Jackson, and told him that if he would consent "to take elucidations on the subject [of West Florida] from me, I will furnish them, and I will make you any acknowledgment." [2] Jackson was a Federalist newspaper man, but he was a patriot, and, perhaps, was somewhat over-nervous as

[1] Madison to Livingston, March 31, 1804, *Am. State Paps.*, *Foreign*, II., 575.
[2] Adams, *United States*, II., 265.

to his personal honor. At all events, he interpreted the last of Yrujo's statements to mean that he would pay any sum of money, within reason no doubt, which he might choose to ask for attacking the Republican administration. The suggestion is made above that Jackson was possibly over-nervous on the subject of his honor, inasmuch as Yrujo, who also was a man of honor, denied that he had any intention of bribing Jackson. The incident is a curious one, because Jackson made a "story" of the attempt to corrupt him, but before printing it sent it to Jefferson, that he might be on his guard and also make any suggestions which might seem desirable. The proposed article came to Monticello in due season, and following closely on it came the Marquis of Casa Yrujo to spend ten days in response to a long-standing invitation. Jefferson treated him with the courtesy of a Virginia gentleman, and, leaving him to enjoy the hospitality of that famous mansion, set out for Washington to consult with his advisers as to what should be done. Yrujo was very angry when he came to a realizing sense that Jefferson and his guests at Monticello — all save himself—were cognizant of this Jackson letter; but he was not angry with himself, as he should have been, for dabbling in newspaper controversies when he was the diplomatic representative of his country. His wrath was directed against Jefferson and Madison, whom he regarded at that moment as no better than a brace of pickpockets.

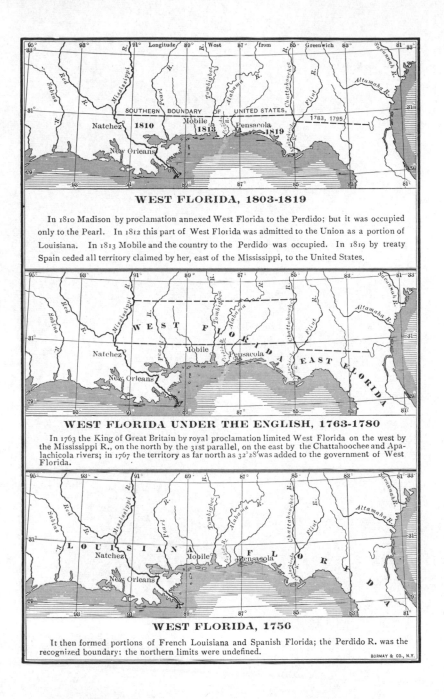

WEST FLORIDA, 1803-1819

In 1810 Madison by proclamation annexed West Florida to the Perdido; but it was occupied only to the Pearl. In 1812 this part of West Florida was admitted to the Union as a portion of Louisiana. In 1813 Mobile and the country to the Perdido was occupied. In 1819 by treaty Spain ceded all territory claimed by her, east of the Mississippi, to the United States.

WEST FLORIDA UNDER THE ENGLISH, 1763-1780

In 1763 the King of Great Britain by royal proclamation limited West Florida on the west by the Mississippi R., on the north by the 31st parallel, on the east by the Chattahoochee and Apalachicola rivers; in 1767 the territory as far north as 32° 28′ was added to the government of West Florida.

WEST FLORIDA, 1756

It then formed portions of French Louisiana and Spanish Florida; the Perdido R. was the recognized boundary: the northern limits were undefined.

BORMAY & CO., N.Y.

Yrujo's indignation, which had been aroused by the sale of Louisiana and strengthened by the claim that the purchase included as much of West Florida as had once formed a part of Louisiana, was brought to the boiling-point by what is generally known as the Mobile Act (February, 1804). This law[1] authorized the president to erect the shores, waters, and inlets of the bay and river of Mobile and neighboring streams into a customs district. The act also provided that the territory ceded to the United States by the Louisiana purchase, and also the navigable waters lying within the United States which empty into the Gulf of Mexico east of the river Mississippi, should be added to the Mississippi district. Yrujo, when the Mobile Act was about two weeks old, entered the state department with a copy of it in his hand and reproached Madison, and requested that the act should be annulled. This, of course, could not be done, and Jefferson issued a proclamation (May 20, 1804), erecting so much of the disputed waters and shores as were within the boundaries of the United States into a collection district.[2]

The United States, in its early years, and possibly even later, seems to have been regarded by foreign governments in the light of a training-school for diplomats and a good place of residence for second-

[1] *Laws of the United States*, VII., 34 (Acts of 1 Sess., 8 Cong., chap. xiii., sec. 11); *U. S. Statutes at Large*, II., 254.

[2] Richardson, *Messages and Papers*, I., 369.

rate persons whose absence from Europe for the moment was greatly to be desired. Such a one was Louis Marie Turreau, the slayer of the Vendeans. Turreau recognized Napoleon as the rightful and inevitable ruler, but was anxious to get away from France, which, indeed, at that time, was not an altogether safe place of residence for revolutionary generals. Besides, it is also said that General Turreau was anxious to escape from his wife. If this were so, the plot did not succeed, as she followed him to America and there fought with him without ceasing. The erstwhile destroyer of the Vendeans had had no experience in diplomacy, no taste for it, could not speak English, and hated America. Nevertheless, he proved to be a faithful servant of his master and a picturesque object in such society as there was at Washington. His reports to Talleyrand, portions of which are printed in Adams's second and third volumes, are very interesting reading, and show that Turreau, notwithstanding his temper and his up-bringing, was a keen observer and had a good deal of common-sense.

Spain, fortunately for us, or we should never have got Louisiana, was under the hand of France. It therefore fell to the lot of General Turreau to endeavor to patch up a peace of some kind between the Marquis of Casa Yrujo and the secretary of state. It was unfortunate that the negotiations with Spain could not be carried on at Washington, for the triumvirate—Jefferson, Madison, and Gallatin—

embodied a deal of solid wisdom coupled with the wiliness of the fox. The American minister at Madrid at the moment was Charles Pinckney, of South Carolina, whose appointment was the price of Jefferson's election in 1800, as Charles Pinckney by his labor with the South Carolina legislators had, to all intents and purposes, made that possible. Jefferson had a Tudor-like memory which made him singularly oblivious to past service when the need of the servant was gone. By this time he had lost all faith in Pinckney, and the vote of South Carolina was no longer necessary, and he had possibly forgotten all about the vicissitudes of 1800. A few years later,[1] in a letter to Monroe, he said there is "a great sense of the inadequacy of C. Pinckney to the office that he is in." At the time of his appointment, Jefferson thought that nothing would induce Pinckney to stay long at his post, but now he does not drop the least hint of a voluntary return. The president, therefore, implored Monroe[2] to avail himself of Pinckney's vanity, expectations, fears, and whatever will weigh with him to induce him to ask leave to return, and declared that he ought to come home to vindicate himself from the charges which his enemies are constantly making against him. Jefferson, indeed, affects solicitude for Pinckney's political future if he does not immediately return to the United States.

[1] Jefferson, *Writings* (Ford's ed.), VIII., 289.
[2] *Ibid.*, VIII., 289.

No one could have wrested West Florida from Spain by diplomatic means, for the Spaniards had been touched in their pride—even Godoy, the Prince of Peace, had become insensible to bribes. Pinckney tried to work on their fears. Acting partly on instructions from Madison and partly on his own initiative, he tried to force West Florida from the Spanish government, and to make them pay spoliation claims for which they denied any responsibility. In the days of the trouble with France at the close of the Federalist epoch, the Spaniards had seized the opportunity to capture American vessels, and had also permitted French privateers to seize American ships in Spanish waters, and had furthermore allowed French consuls to condemn these luckless American ships in prize-courts sitting in Spanish towns. Finally, the closure of the Mississippi in 1802 had brought financial loss to many Americans for which an indemnity might be exacted. Spain agreed to pay the first set of claims, but refused to admit her liability for the actions of the French; she had done what she could to protect her neutrality, and the French had paid no attention to her wishes. Pinckney accepted what he could get, embodied the terms in a convention, and sent it to the United States for ratification, with the suggestion that it would better be ratified and used as a basis for pressing the other claims. Ratification was delayed for two years, and when the convention reappeared in Spain the Spaniards refused to ratify.

Pinckney threatened; he declared that if the Spaniards continued contumacious he would shut up the legation and leave Spain. They took him at his word, and he continued at Madrid.[1]

It was while affairs were in this disagreeable trim that the favorite diplomatist of the Jeffersonian party appeared at Madrid and undertook to bring the stiff-necked Dons to reason. In appointing him to France, Spain, and England, Jefferson had informed Monroe that he had been "born for the public," and had been fitted by nature for the service of the human race on a broad scale, and had been stamped with the evidences of his destination and his duty, but Jefferson did not accurately define the ear-marks of a presidential candidate.[2] These were not evident to Robert R. Livingston, although he seems to have been conscious that Monroe was highly favored by the administration and to have done what he could to lessen Monroe's influence. We find him, for instance, not long after his famous interview with Marbois, writing to Madison a letter which plainly implied that he was conducting the negotiation alone. Monroe, on his part, informed Madison or Jefferson, or both of them, that Napoleon, hearing of his arrival at Paris, made the offer to sell Louisiana.[3] Livingston and Mon-

---

[1] *Am. State Paps., Foreign*, II., 613–624; Adams, *United States*, II., 284.

[2] Jefferson, *Writings* (Ford's ed.), VIII., 191.

[3] For Monroe's side of the case, see his *Writings*, IV., 135, 148.

roe were well aware of each other's feelings, although probably neither was conscious of the extent to which the other had gone for the purpose of undermining a possible rival for the presidency or some very high office. It fell out in this way that when Monroe appeared in Paris on his way from London to Madrid that Livingston did not feel disposed to further his wishes more than was absolutely necessary. Armstrong had also arrived at Paris as the accredited minister to France, but he had not been received, so that Livingston was still in control of the situation.

Monroe's idea was to approach the Spaniards with the backing of the French government. He sought Talleyrand, but that astute gentleman did not respond to his advances in a kindly spirit, while Livingston told him that he had no business to seek interviews with the French minister of foreign affairs. Feeling nervous over the result of his proposed journey, Monroe determined to have one more interview with the sphinx of French diplomacy. He sought Talleyrand's residence alone. When he arrived there he found a line of carriages in the street outside, and, applying at the door, was informed that a reception of ambassadors was going forward. The door - keeper suggested that he might ask his master as to whether the new guest should be admitted, but Monroe thought that he would better not intrude. In the end he departed for Madrid without having received any answer to his last communication to Talleyrand.[1]

Arriving at Madrid, Monroe soon discovered that the luckless Pinckney had done the only possible thing. The Prince of Peace had got his back to the wall — war or peace seemed to be quite indifferent to him — the control of the destinies of Spain had passed out of his hands. The correspondence was carried on with Don Pedro de Cevallos, who acted as a sort of head clerk in foreign affairs. He drew Monroe out until Godoy had received his instructions from France. When they came, the Spaniard made it clear that he would not cede Florida, would not ratify the convention, would not do anything except to be unpleasant. Monroe shook the dust of Madrid from his shoes, leaving the hapless Pinckney with still some months of Spanish indignities to endure.[2]

General Armstrong had now taken possession at Paris. He wrote to Monroe that the best thing for the United States to do would be to march a strong body of troops to the extreme southern limit of Texas and take prompt and effectual possession of that portion of the Louisiana purchase which France had practically acknowledged to belong to the United States. "A stroke of this kind would at once bring Spain to reason and France to her rescue,

---

[1] Adams, *United States*, II., chap. xiii.
[2] Monroe's account of this episode in his life is given in a letter to Madison, in Monroe, *Writings*, IV., 303.

and without giving either room to quarrel." [1] The
president, then, might shape the bargain as to Florida
pretty much as he wished. This was undoubtedly
the soundest advice that was given in the time of
this imbroglio; but it was diametrically opposed
to the idea, which had been formerly set forth by
both Livingston and Monroe, and upheld by Jefferson and Madison, that West Florida to the Perdido
was included within the limits of the Louisiana purchase.

Nearly four months after the date of this letter,
Armstrong wrote in quite a different tone to the
secretary of state, enclosing a memorandum in Talleyrand's handwriting, but without any signature.
This note proposed that the United States should
reopen negotiations with Spain, and should suggest that Spain join with the United States in referring the whole matter in dispute with Spain
to the decision of Napoleon. If Spain, on his advice, should consent to part with the Floridas, the
United States might give up the extreme southern
portion of Texas, pay ten million dollars to Spain,
and take Spanish colonial bills in payment of claims
of American citizens against Spain, excluding those
which involved France. Armstrong demurred to
the high price which the United States would have
to pay under this arrangement, and the person who
brought the memorandum to him suggested that the

[1] Adams, *United States*, III., 39, from MSS. in the state department.

ten million dollars might be reduced to seven million dollars. He also called attention to the fact that the claims of the United States against Spain amounted to nearly three million dollars, which would leave the actual sum to be paid out of the American treasury to Spain at a little over four million dollars. Armstrong transmitted the memorandum[1] to Madison, and it turned the wavering minds of the president and the secretary of state.

Jefferson realized that in the Louisiana purchase France had sold to the United States a portion of Spanish America and then had compelled Spain to acquiesce in this disposal of Spanish property. It seemed to him that this memorandum was an invitation to do the same thing over again as to Florida. He therefore talked of preparations for war, and made preparations for peace. In his fifth annual message[2] to Congress (December 3, 1805), he recounted that propositions for adjusting amicably the boundaries of Louisiana had not been acceded to. On the contrary, inroads had been made "into the Territories of Orleans and the Mississippi." The president had, therefore, found it necessary to order troops to the frontier to repel by force of arms any similar aggressions in the future. Some of the injuries which he noted clearly could be met only by force. He therefore recommended such preparations as circumstances called for to protect the sea-

---

[1] Adams, *United States*, III., 105, from MSS. in the state department.   [2] Richardson, *Messages and Papers*, I., 382.

ports, to extend the gunboat service, to organize or class the militia, and to provide a military force which could be called upon in any sudden emergency. He declared that the last census showed the United States to contain upward of three hundred thousand men between the ages of eighteen and twenty-six years. He stated that considerable provision had been made towards the collection of materials for the construction of ships of war of seventy-four guns. In this time of "violence and wrong" he advised the immediate prohibition of the exportation of arms and ammunition.

Jefferson seemed to have definitely abandoned himself to what he described as the Quaker policy of turning the other cheek to the smiter. Indeed, every one was expecting war when, three days later, another message came to the House of Representatives, which was considered behind closed doors. In this secret message [1] Jefferson adverted at some length to the history of the dispute with Spain, and then, turning to France, stated that there was reason to believe that the latter country was disposed to effect a settlement so comprehensive as to remove the grounds of future controversy on the eastern side of the Mississippi as well as on the western side. The present crisis in Europe is favorable to this settlement. Formal war is not necessary, but the course to be pursued will require the command of means which must be provided

[1] Richardson *Messages and Papers*, I., 388.

by Congress. Randolph, as chairman of the committee of ways and means, was expected to move the
appropriation of two million dollars as "provision for
the purchase of Florida." Gallatin handed a paper
with this title to Randolph, and Jefferson confided
to the care of Joseph Nicholson, who was a kinsman
of Gallatin's wife, several resolutions which he had
drawn and which Nicholson was expected to move,
as General Smith had moved similar resolutions in
the days of 1803.[1]

The days of 1803 were no more. Gallatin might
be the intermediary, but Randolph, who had seen
nothing immoral in the Louisiana matter, saw in
this transaction the hand of the Yazoo men, more
especially that of James Madison. He turned upon
the administration and said that the president must
ask openly for the money, and that Congress would
not deliver the "public purse to the first cutthroat
that demanded it." The administration forces rallied to the support of the president, and the bill
was passed by a vote of 76 to 54.[2] But the delay
was fatal, the answer reached Armstrong six months
after the date of his letter—too late to be of service.
Either Talleyrand had acted without authority, or
Napoleon had made one of his sudden changes of
mind, and in the interval had come to the conclusion to seize the Spanish monarchy, colonies and all.

[1] See above, p. 64.
[2] *Laws of the United States*, VIII., 7 (Acts of 1 Sess., 9 Cong.,
chap. v.); *U. S. Statutes at Large*, II., 349.

Whatever the true explanation of the Florida intrigue may be, one fact stands out clearly, and that is that for Thomas Jefferson the "harvest season" was ended.

CHAPTER XII

THE BURR EXPEDITION

(1805–1807)

AARON BURR returned to Washington in time to preside at the impeachment trial of Samuel Chase. He then relinquished the vice-president's chair to his successful rival in New York politics, George Clinton. An outcast in New Jersey, New York, and New England, Burr travelled about the country as far west as the Mississippi River. He lived, while in the east, mainly at Washington and Philadelphia. His life for the next few years is still shrouded in mystery, and will probably always remain so. His stories and those of his companions in conspiracy were so various and were so differently interpreted by those who listened to them that it is impossible to say precisely what credit can be given to the several classes of evidence.

On his first visit to the west, in 1805, Burr was received with attention, as the retiring vice-president naturally would be. He was entertained with great cordiality by Andrew Jackson, major-general of the Tennessee militia, who probably saw in the former companion of the dashing soldier Benedict Arnold

and the successful duellist a man of his own kind,
albeit more educated and more worldly. What
Burr said to Jackson will never be known. One
thing is certain: Jackson was too straightforward
and honest a man to read into Burr's conversation
anything treasonable or dishonorable which was not
plainly so on the face of it. Another man whom he
met in the west was a person of very different stamp.
This was an old companion in arms of the Revolutionary War, James Wilkinson, who now commanded the little United States army which was stationed
in the Mississippi Valley. Wilkinson is one of the
problematical characters of history. He first comes
into notice in the Revolution, in the Conway Cabal.[1]
From that time on he mixed in nearly every doubtful transaction which occurred within reach of his
place of residence, and cast a halo of mystery
about his part in the play. He was, or had been,
a pensioner of Spain, and now became involved in
Burr's scheme, but exactly to what extent is not
known. After visiting Wilkinson, Burr descended
the Mississippi to New Orleans, where he made the
acquaintance of Daniel Clark, the leading American
merchant in that region. Living in the focus of
Spanish intrigue, Daniel Clark had the happy fac-
ulty of having a finger in most of them without
being inextricably involved in any one of them.

[1] Wilkinson, *Memoirs of My Own Times*, gives his own estimate of his career; but it is one of the most unreliable books of
its class.

Burr then returned to the east and carried on his
projects more openly. His eastern partner was
Jonathan Dayton, once Federalist speaker of the
national House of Representatives and later senator from New Jersey.

What Burr had in mind is not clear to us and possibly was not clear to him. He was restive and ambi-
tious, of vivid imagination, with everything to gain
and nothing except his life and liberty to lose. If
we may believe the stories which the Marquis of
Casa Yrujo wrote to his government, and those
which Anthony Merry sent to his superiors at London,[1] Burr's plan was something like the following:
He thought that he saw discontent in Louisiana, dis-
satisfaction in Kentucky and Tennessee, and possibly in Ohio, and disaffection in New England. He
had been cognizant of the Federalist plans for the
withdrawal of New England from the Union; he now
thought that New England might at any time secede.
With some money and possibly military help from
either England or Spain, the American settlers west
of the mountains might likewise be induced to withdraw from the Union. This would leave the middle
states and the southern states as the only reliance
for the administration. It is not impossible that at
one time Burr, in an indefinite and hazy way, may

[1] This aspect of the Burr problem has been very fully treated
by Henry Adams (*History of the United States*, III., chap. x.).
As is natural with a discoverer of documents, Adams probably
places an undue importance on those he has printed from the
English and Spanish archives.

have contemplated kidnapping the president and the higher officers of the government. These ideas may be regarded as representing Burr's dreams in their widest aspect. That he ever seriously contemplated carrying into execution anything of the kind is highly improbable.

The instability of Burr's imagination induced in him lightning-like changes of plan—he was an opportunist in conspiracy. Another form of the enterprise, therefore, contemplated the revolutionizing of Mexico and the possible annexation to the new state of portions of the Louisiana purchase. Since Burr and Dayton were sadly in want of funds, the form which the scheme took at any one moment depended very largely upon the person with whom Burr and Dayton happened to be talking at the moment, and the probability of that person providing money for their depleted cash-boxes. For example, when the Spaniards seemed complaisant, something advantageous for Spain was represented as being on foot which might well be furthered by the payment of Spanish money. At other times, when Spain seemed to be unfriendly, the project took on the form of an attack on Spanish territory which could best be prevented by the payment of money to Burr and Dayton. To the English ministry great hopes were held out of the establishment of a new government in the Gulf region which would be friendly to British commercial interests. This plan had more promise than the scheme of Spanish

aid, because the British treasury was better filled
than was that of Spain; but Pitt's sudden death
and the accession to power of Charles James Fox
resulted in the absolute downfall of any hope of
British money and in the sudden recall of Anthony
Merry.[1]

As it was, in the summer of 1806, with little
money and no powerful confederates, Burr crossed
the Alleghanies and pushed on preparations for
bringing his scheme, whatever it was, to a successful conclusion. On an island in the Ohio River,
he visited an eccentric Irish gentleman, Harman
Blennerhassett by name. This man had expended
one-half of his property in converting his island into
a species of wilderness paradise. The income from
the remainder of his property was by no means sufficient to keep his paradise in good condition. He
was, therefore, extremely desirous of finding some
quick and easy road to wealth. Burr proposed to
him that together they should buy a great land claim
in Louisiana. The title to this land was not clear,
but if Burr's plan succeeded it might be feasible to
make firm what was a doubtful claim when purchased. Blennerhassett embarked in the venture
and paid over some thousands of dollars, but he
received certain guarantees from Burr's son-in-law,
Joseph Alston, who was reputed to be the richest

[1] It is interesting to compare McCaleb's views of this part of
the Burr problem with those of Adams as noted above; see
McCaleb, *The Aaron Burr Conspiracy*, chap. iii.

planter in South Carolina. Some of this money was used to pay for land, a fact which goes far to confirm the belief that Burr's schemes may have been nothing more than a great land-jobbing undertaking, with an attack on Mexico in case the United States should speedily become involved in war with Spain.[1]

For a year and a half Jefferson refused to believe that there was anything serious behind the stories which were constantly brought to him of Burr's proposed undertaking. It would have been well for all concerned had the president continued to cling to his faith in the patriotism of the western people and in their good sense. It happened otherwise, however, for when Burr began to build boats to carry his parties down the Ohio and Mississippi rivers, the politicians of Kentucky and Tennessee and of Ohio bestirred themselves to make whatever capital they could out of the incident. Having made arrangements for the building of his flotilla and the embarkation of his men, Burr left Blennerhassett's Island and journeyed to Tennessee, with a view, mainly it seems, to raise more men and if possible to enlist the services of Andrew Jackson. It fell out in this way, therefore, that Burr was some two hundred miles away when the only thing was done which could be regarded as an overt act of levying

[1] See, on this point, McCaleb, *The Aaron Burr Conspiracy*, passim. The evidence given at Burr's trial (Robertson, *Reports of the Trials of Aaron Burr*) seems to point in the same direction.

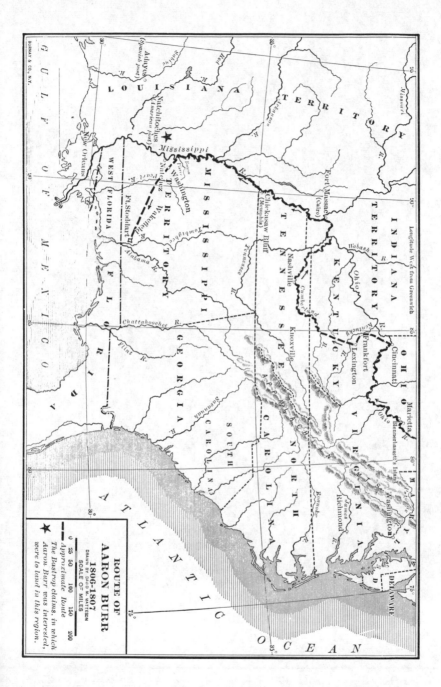

ROUTE OF
AARON BURR
1806-1807
DRAWN BY DAVID B. MATTESON
SCALE OF MILES
0 25 50   100   150   200

▬ ▬ Approximate Route
★   The Bastrop claims, in which
      Aaron Burr was interested,
      were to lead in this region.

war against the United States.   In the end the preparations had to be cut short, and instead of the force
of five hundred men which Burr had talked about,
only sixty in five boats drifted away from Blennerhassett's Island, and were finally joined by Burr near
where the town of Cairo now stands.[1]

Meantime, at New Orleans and in western Louisiana, all was confusion.   In New Orleans the creoles
were greatly dissatisfied at the arrangements which
had been made for their government, and their discontent took on the form of dislike and distrust of
Governor Claiborne.   On his part, Claiborne, who
did not speak either Spanish or French, felt a distrust of those about him whom he could not understand, and was uneasy in the mystery which surrounded him, but which he could not penetrate.
Daniel Clark and the leading men in New Orleans
were well informed of the movements of Burr.
There had also come to the creole capital Dayton
and two of Burr's less-important agents, who had
sailed around from New York while Burr was drift-
ing down-stream.   These brought a letter from Burr
to Clark, in which the latter was assured that everything was all right.   This assurance was greatly
needed, for Clark and his friends had no confidence
in Burr's ability to carry out his plans.

While Burr was in Tennessee, Jefferson issued a

---

[1] Adams, *United States*, III., chap. xii.; McCaleb, *The Aaron
Burr Conspiracy*, chap. ix.; Davis, *Memoirs of Aaron Burr*, II.,
chaps. xx., xxi.

proclamation reciting that sundry persons were con-
spiring to set on foot a military enterprise against
the dominions of Spain contrary to the laws, and
warning all good citizens against participating in
the expedition. He further called upon them to
arrest the offenders and prevent their design. The
heads of the executive departments also brought
the matter directly to the notice of their subordinates
and issued the necessary orders. The proclamation[1]
was dated November 27, 1806. It took an uncon-
scionable amount of time for it to be carried to the
posts on the line of Burr's route. The result was
that he was able to leave Tennessee, reach Fort
Massac, and even confer peaceably with Captain
Bissell, the commander of that post. This interview
was held thirty-two days after the date of the proclamation, which, indeed, occupied forty days on the
way, while a letter that Bissell wrote to Jackson
and the latter forwarded to the government occupied
only twenty-three days in going up-stream and
thence to Washington. Who was responsible for the
delay which enabled Burr to pass Fort Massac was
not ascertained at the time and is not now known.
Burr clearly had sympathizers among the frontier
settlers, and the soldiers of the garrison on the river
would gladly have left their posts and gone with him.
They suspected nothing treasonable in his designs,
nor did so patriotic men as Andrew Jackson and

[1] *Annals of Cong.*, 9 Cong., 2 Sess., 686; Richardson, *Messages and Papers*, I., 404.

Henry Clay.   As it was, Burr secured a furlough for
one of the sergeants at Fort Massac.   At Chickasaw
Bluffs, where Memphis now stands, was another
United States military post.   The commander at
that place had received no depreciatory word as
to Burr.   He would have liked to join Aaron Burr,
but, as that was impossible, he undertook to raise a
company for him and send it on after him.   What
story the ex-vice-president told these two men, who
were faithful officers of the army, is not known; it
evidently satisfied them as to Burr's patriotism and
purpose.   Proceeding down-stream, the expedition
in due season reached Natchez, and there was
stopped owing to the action of General Wilkinson,
upon whose aid or connivance Burr had relied, and
who had pronounced against him.

No part of Wilkinson's mysterious and problematical career is more mysterious and problematical
than his action at this time.   He commanded the
military forces of the United States in the west and
southwest; he alone could stop Burr or could give
success to his plans.   Wilkinson, Burr, and Dayton
had been long in correspondence, but Burr had
never told Wilkinson what his plans really were.
They had written him many letters, but those letters,
so far as they have been preserved, convey little
specific information.

At this juncture Spanish troops appeared in Texas
and marched into territory which was clearly included in the Louisiana purchase.   It is possible

that this activity on the part of the Mexican army was designed for defence in case the government at Washington should adopt Armstrong's suggestion, which has been noted on a preceding page, and should occupy Texas to the Rio Grande. There is no clear proof on this point, however; it may be that the Spaniards advanced eastward of the Sabine River in consequence of Burr's and Dayton's dealings with the Marquis of Casa Yrujo; or, possibly, they knew Burr's real design. At all events, Wilkinson massed his little force to oppose the Spaniards, and these, in consequence of his activity, retired from their most eastern positions.

Wilkinson, therefore, was at the extreme southwestern limit of his command when one of Burr's messengers, who had come to New Orleans by sea, brought him a letter from the ex-vice-president. A man with Wilkinson's experience in intrigue, on perusing this epistle, must have felt that Burr was not dealing fairly with him. Any unprejudiced observer must admit that Wilkinson's position was full of peril. In front of him was a Spanish force capable of giving him a good deal of trouble; behind him was New Orleans, full of disaffected Spaniards and Frenchmen; and Burr was descending the Mississippi with an armed force, nearly as numerous as his own. Surely any commander so circumstanced might well have acted only after due deliberation with himself and after consultation with his officers. Had Wilkinson's character been good, and had he not been deeply involved in Burr's schemes, little fault could be found with the measures which he took to safeguard the interests of his superiors. He entered into an arrangement with the Spanish commander which obviated danger from that quarter for the time being; he then moved nearly all his soldiers to New Orleans, which was the real danger spot. There he probably acted with undue harshness and with a display of unnecessary authority; but he knew a great deal more of the circumstances than we do at the present day.[1]

Meantime, Burr, descending the Mississippi, had landed near Natchez and had received information which showed him that the further prosecution of his plan was hopeless. He surrendered to the commander at Natchez, but managed to sink in the river the cases containing his arms. The inhabitants of that part of Mississippi territory, ignoring what was alleged against Burr, sympathized with what they understood to be the object of his expedition. The grand jurors not only refused to indict Burr, they presented his arrest as a grievance. Burr made the best of the respite which was thus obtained. He disguised himself, deserted his companions, and disappeared into the wilderness. A month later, when almost within sight of the boundary of Spanish Florida, he was recognized and arrested by the commanding officer of Fort Stoddert, the most southern American station on the Mobile

[1] Wilkinson, *Memoirs of My Own Times*, II., chaps. viii., ix.

River. Thence he was taken overland to Richmond, Virginia, and tried for his life on a charge of treason.[1]

It would have been well had Burr succeeded in passing Fort Stoddert and finding refuge within the Spanish lines, for the trial which followed, in itself and in its result, was not a commendable episode in the history of the United States. Chief-Justice John Marshall presided as circuit judge, and gave the weight of his great name to the summoning of the president of the United States to appear in court and place himself at the mercy of attorneys who were defending an accused traitor. He not only did this, but, in deciding that the application of Burr's attorneys should be granted, made statements that could not help being unpleasant to the chief executive. He also appointed a personal enemy of Jefferson, John Randolph of Roanoke, as foreman of the jury. Jefferson, on his side, lost control of himself for a season. He very properly declined to appear as a witness; but he went beyond this and hounded on the persecution of Burr. He even proposed, in a moment of great irritation, that Luther Martin, "this unprincipled & impudent federal bull-dog" who defended Burr, should be committed for misprision of treason, if not as being an actual participant with Burr.[2]

[1] McCaleb, *The Aaron Burr Conspiracy*, 279.

[2] Jefferson to Hay, June 19, 1807, Jefferson, *Writings* (Ford's ed.), IX., 58 *n.*; there are many letters in this volume on the Burr incident, showing how deeply Jefferson was excited by the treatment meted out to him by the Federalists.

The principal witness at the trial was General
James Wilkinson. So much doubt attached to his
own part in the affair that he doubtless felt it necessary to carry the thing through with a certain degree of grandeur which was quite in keeping with
his character. The most creditable point in his career, indeed, is the astonishing fact that the "federal bull-dog" and his able associates, who were
carefully advised by Burr, himself no mean lawyer,
could not convict Wilkinson out of his own mouth
of misdemeanor and perjury.[1]

It made little difference what evidence could be
brought against Burr, for the chief-justice decided
that under none of the circumstances of the case
could the ex-vice-president be convicted of treason.
Treason, under the Constitution, required an overt
act of levying war or giving aid and comfort to the
enemies of the United States. Burr had been two
hundred miles away when the only thing occurred
which could be twisted into an overt act of war
by any reasoning. According to John Marshall, a
man could not commit an overt act who was not
actually present in the flesh at the time and place
of the levying of war. His might be the brain
which had devised the plot, his might be the resources which had provided the muskets with which
war was levied—if he were not present when the

[1] See David Robertson, *Reports of the Trials of Colonel Aaron
Burr (late Vice-President of the United States), for Treason and
for a Misdemeanor* (1808).

muskets were used, he did not commit an overt act. Burr was discharged. For four years he lived in Europe. He then returned to New York, and there lived and died in obscurity in 1836.[1] The outcome of Burr's trial made Jefferson feel more convinced than before of the malignancy of his fellow-Virginian John Marshall.

[1] See *The Private Journal of Aaron Burr, Reprinted in Full from the Original Manuscript* (2 vols., 1903). Davis gives a modified version in his *Memoirs of Burr*, II., chap. xxii.; in chap. xxiii. he summarizes what is known of Burr's later life.

CHAPTER XIII

FOREIGN RELATIONS

(1805)

THE main interest in Jefferson's first administration was the application of Republican principles to the solution of problems of domestic polity; the guiding force during the second administration was the foreign relations of the United States. The time was one of peculiar difficulty: Great Britain and France, with their attendant allies and tributary states, were striving for each other's lifeblood. France became predominant on the continent of Europe; England gained the supremacy of the seas. Each power was triumphant in its sphere. The only mode by which either of them could further annoy the other, unless the other were foolish enough to forsake its peculiar place, was by inflicting upon it the torments of starvation. This the contending parties sought to accomplish by putting an end to all trade with the other nation. The United States was then the principal neutral commercial country. Upon it, therefore, fell the weight of this new mode of warfare. Jefferson brought to the management of this difficult problem the same political shrewdness with which he had forced his way into power; but the elements against which he now contended were very different from those which he had hitherto successfully confronted. The European combatants proved deaf to the resources of philosophy and hunger. Jefferson's exhortations and his appeal to their pocket-books were both without avail. It is true that the suffering of English people and the dictates of human reason ultimately impelled the English government to yield. But by that time the control of events in America had slipped from the hands of the Jeffersonians, and war was declared at almost the moment when the British receded from the position which they long had held.

The elements in this three-cornered conflict were various. To gain an understanding of the form which it took, it will be necessary to turn back to the preceding century to gather the various threads which made up this tangled skein. Two general lines of action will reveal themselves, one having to do with the question of impressment; the other relating to the rights of neutrals on the high seas and on the coasts of warring nations.

All European nations in the eighteenth century were united in holding to the doctrine of indefeasible allegiance; once a Frenchman, always a Frenchman; once an Englishman, always an Englishman. The United States occupied an anomalous position in that it was a state in the international acceptance of the word, and at the same time had many of the attributes of its former existence as a group of colonies. The American nation was made up of divers races. It had grown by natural increase and by constant accessions from England and the continent. As one way to induce foreigners to seek American shores, a liberal policy had prevailed, even before the Revolution, of conferring political rights upon all foreign Protestants who settled in the country and gave evidence of becoming permanent residents in the colonies.

This policy was contained in several acts of Parliament; it was amplified and extended by colonial legislation. The period of residence required in the parliamentary naturalization laws was ordinarily five years, but the colonial legislatures gave civil rights in their respective colonies after much briefer periods. Sometimes, indeed, rights of citizenship in a colony were conferred upon new-comers almost upon their arrival; occasionally bands of especially desirable immigrants were naturalized before they left their homes in Germany. The laws of the United States and of the several states merely continued the arrangements which had been established in colonial days. In England, on the other hand, naturalization still continued to depend on special acts of Parliament. It fell out in this way that the regular practice of Great Britain and of the United States had become so different that complications were certain to arise unless great forbearance was displayed by both Englishmen and Americans.

Conscription was at the basis of the military systems of the continent. In England there was technically nothing of the kind, but the navy was manned, to a considerable extent, by persons who were forced into the service by a process which was known as impressment. The discipline on British naval ships was harsh, the conditions as to food and clothing were undesirable, and the labor required was arduous. The naval service was unpopular among seamen. Wages were high and the treatment was good on American merchant-men. British seamen fled from English ships and embarked on American vessels. It is impossible to state how many sailors of English, Scottish, and Irish birth were serving on American merchant-ships; the number is given in contemporary writings as high as thirty or forty thousand, which is doubtless a gross exaggeration.[1] That there were many British seamen on American ships was made clear at the time of the embargo, when several hundred of them were stranded in New York and other seaports, and preferred transportation to Halifax with the certainty of service in the English navy to performing such labor às was necessary to keep body and soul together on land. To complicate matters still more, British seamen deserted from British naval vessels,

[1] *Barclay Correspondence*, 274; see also *ibid.*, 132, and Gallatin, *Works* (Adams's ed.), I., 335, Gallatin's report. The *Boston Centinel* of September 24, 1808, gives the whole number of seamen in the United States as 65,000, of whom 48,000 belonged to New England and New York.

procured naturalization papers or certificates of citizenship, and derided the officers of the ships from
which they escaped. The English naval officers of
that time were naturally inflated by the size and
strength of the British navy and by the victories
which British ships constantly won over those of
France and Spain. These officers were overbearing
in their manners and were dictatorial in their language. They could hardly be expected to quietly
pace their quarter-decks and see American ships
go sailing by with full crews, half or two-thirds of
which were English born, without an attempt to secure recruits for their own depleted numbers.

There was something to be said on their side of
the case. Taxes in England were heavy, the cus-
tom of impressment had come down from the
olden time when the king required the personal
service of his subjects in time of war. Since the
day when Medina Sidonia sailed up the channel
with his "felicissima armada," England had not
been in such danger as she was from the world-
conquering desire of Napoleon Bonaparte; then, if
ever, England might expect every Englishman to
do his duty. The peace of Amiens in 1802 found
the question of impressment undecided between
England and America; the renewal of the conflict
between England and France witnessed a revival
of the activity of the English press gangs and of
the forcing American citizens, both native-born and
naturalized, to the decks of English men-of-war.

The anger of English merchants and statesmen was aroused, not merely by the belief that thousands of English seamen were on American ships, but by the thought that there were so many American ships on which their seamen could find shelter.[1] In the old days before the American Revolution the colonists, especially those of New England, New York, Pennsylvania, and Maryland, enjoyed their share in the carrying - trade of the British empire. After 1783 American ship-masters and merchants acted as though they expected to continue to enjoy the advantages of the English colonial system without sharing in its burdens.[2] The English government and merchants had other views; but the exigencies of the situation in the West Indies forced them to permit the Americans to enjoy many of the advantages of colonial trade to which they were not in any way entitled by the colonial systems of European nations. The English West Indian islands produced bountiful crops of sugar and the attendant molasses and rum. Much of the food required by the planters and their slaves had been procured from the continental colonies, as well as some articles of other kinds. The prosperity of the islands required that they should continue to be fed in part

---

[1] James Stephen, *War in Disguise; or, the Frauds of the Neutral Flags;* Alexander Baring, *An Inquiry into the Causes and Consequences of the Orders in Council,* when read together give one a good idea of the English point of view.

[2] McLaughlin, *Confederation and Constitution (Am. Nation,* X.), chap. v.

from the continent. This fact was recognized by the negotiators of the Jay treaty of 1794, which provided for a limited trade between the British West Indian islands and the United States.

Great Britain had not been the only power to monopolize the trade of its colonial possessions; that was the universal practice of the colonizing nations of Europe. As long as there was peace, colonial ports were regularly open only to the vessels of the mother-country; when war came outsiders were admitted. For instance, in the tremendous contest which closed with the peace of Paris of 1763, France found herself driven from the ocean. She could not protect the vessels of her subjects sailing to and from the French islands. To save her planters from ruin she opened her ports to vessels of Spain and Portugal and the Netherlands. The prosperity of the French West Indian planters did not appeal to the English government in the same way; they hit upon the expedient of declaring that commerce which was forbidden in time of peace should not be permitted in time of war, on the ground that such trade was in effect aiding the belligerent. This was known as the "Rule of War of 1756." It operated to prevent a neutral from carrying goods in war time which he could not carry in peaceful days.[1]

In 1793 France and England came to blows. French revolutionary fervor made her armies well-

---

[1] [Madison], *An Examination of the British Doctrine;* Thwaites, *France in America* (*Am. Nation*, VII.), chap. xvi.

nigh irresistible on land, but did not seem to produce the same effect on her seamen in conflict with the impressed sailors of England. France opened her West Indian ports to American vessels. They also enjoyed a portion of the carrying - trade of British West Indian islands. Under the twofold stimulus, the American merchant marine increased with marvellous rapidity, greatly to the disgust of English ship-owners and merchants. The Rule of War of 1756 was once more invoked; but this time a way around it was discovered. This was to carry the products of a French, Spanish, or Dutch West Indian island to an American port, land the cargo, pay the customs duties, reship it, and sail with new clearance papers for a port of the mother-country. English naval officers soon interfered with this prosperous commerce. The matter came before the English admiralty courts. In a series of luminous decisions Sir William Scott, who is better known by his later title of Lord Stowell, laid down the general doctrine which permitted this commerce. In the case of the *Immanuel* [1] (1799) he declared that when the produce of a colony became part of the national stock of the neutral country, it might be carried from the neutral country to the ports of the mother-land. In the case of the *Polly* [2] (1800) he held that landing the goods and paying the duty were

---

[1] Robinson, *Admiralty Reports*, II., 186; Bassett, *Federalist System* (*Am. Nation*, XI.), chap. viii.
[2] Robinson, *Admiralty Reports*, II., 361.

evidence that the produce had been incorporated in the national stock.

The complaisant attitude of the English government at this time was no doubt due in part to the disagreement between the United States and France. For the moment Americans were fighting the battles of England. Never in the early history of the United States under the Constitution were relations with England in a more favorable condition than they were at the accession of President Jefferson. He made every effort to ingratiate himself with the British government. A keen writer has said that Jefferson took his color from the locality in which he happened to be at any particular moment. When he came to Washington and assumed the duties of his office, he found the government disbanding the forces which had been brought together for a naval conflict with France. He met Thornton, the English secretary of legation, whom Liston had left in charge, and told him that he was aware that he had been represented as hostile to Great Britain; but this, he said, had been done only for electioneering purposes, and he hoped that such language would be used no longer. This was before the inauguration; after that event he reopened the subject, and said that he had at heart the adjustment of all differences between the two countries. He admitted that for republican France he had felt some interest, but that there was nothing in the present government of that country to induce him

to show the least partiality.[1]   The years passed on;
Louisiana fell into the hands of the surprised Jefferson; there was no longer thought of an English
alliance.   With the reopening of the war of 1803,
Jefferson determined to adopt a stronger tone towards Great Britain on the subject of impressment
and the right of search.   The first indication of
this changed policy was in the treatment which he
meted out to Anthony Merry.

Of all the underbred Englishmen of moderate
capacity whom the rulers of Great Britain have
first and last sent to Washington, Anthony Merry
was the least well-bred and among the stupidest.
He was a slow, excessively English Englishman with
a very punctilious wife.   Jefferson had had long experience in public life: for four years he had represented the United States at the court of France,
for four years he had performed the duties of secretary of state in the administration of Washington.
He knew the requirements of official and diplomatic
intercourse as thoroughly as any man in the United
States.   Jefferson, however, had been born on the
frontier, had grown up in the wilderness, and combined with the freedom of thought and action
which these early surroundings gave him the somewhat despotic manners of a Virginia gentleman.
Under his rule the White House was open to all

---

[1] See letters from Edward Thornton, British *chargé* at Washington, to Grenville and Hawkesbury, in Adams, *United States*,
II., 343, 348.

comers as was his own residence of Monticello on his distant Virginia hill-top.

Up to this time he had put a certain amount of restraint upon his natural inclinations, but apparently the coming of Mr. Merry seemed to him to be a good opportunity to lay down a new policy in the foreign relations of the United States as exemplified in social customs, and especially to show the representative of England some of that want of consideration which the American minister at London constantly found to be his portion. He therefore drew up a paper entitled "Canons of Etiquette to be Observed by the Executive."[1] For the time to come, all guests at the White House were to be on a footing of equality. This idea was not new to Jefferson. In 1788 he had suggested that in a new country etiquette might well be based on natural reasons as stature or age.[2] It was unfortunate that the well-meaning but stupid Anthony Merry and his disagreeable wife should have been the first to experience the new etiquette, or lack of it—for they were the last people in the world to understand it. Arrived in Washington, and already vexed at the difficulty of securing suitable quarters, Mr. Merry put on his court costume and repaired with the secretary of state to the White House, where he was

[1] The rough draught is in Jefferson, *Writings* (Ford's ed.), VIII., 276.

[2] Jefferson to Moustier, May 17, 1788; Jefferson, *Writings* (Ford's ed.), V., 10; see also Nathaniel Macon to John Steele, University of North Carolina, *Bulletin*, No. 1, p. 49.

received by the president in faded waistcoat, spotted breeches, and slippers without heels. At a subsequent dinner Jefferson invited both the British minister and the French *chargé* to be present, although France and England were at war. When the doors were opened, he seized the hand of Mrs. Madison, walked into the dining-room, and left the rest of the guests to shift for themselves.

Undoubtedly, Merry made too much of the incident, but he might well have asked what other interpretation could be placed on the doings of an experienced diplomatist like Jefferson than a determination to belittle the position of his Britannic majesty's minister at Washington. At all events, he declared that this treatment was an insult to his country and was so intended. James Monroe, American minister in England at about the same time, attended an official dinner given by Lord Hawkesbury, who at the moment was in charge of the foreign office. On this occasion the ladies went in first, the gentlemen following in a body; but at a later "diplomatic dinner" the guests were arranged in such a manner as to give Monroe the lowest place. At the earlier of these repasts Monroe strove to be discreet and talked about the weather— in the United States. In conclusion, he observed that in Charleston, South Carolina, at the races, the equipages and the people were a very interesting sight. Lord Castlereagh inquired as to the equipages, and Monroe explained that they were similar

to those which one saw every day in London.
Thereupon Sir William Scott declared that the subject reminded him of a description he had read in
a paper published at Cape Town of a local func-
tion at which all "the beauty, taste & fashion of
Africa" had been present.[1]   Monroe did not join in
the general laugh at this sally of the admiralty
judge; but later in the evening he took occasion to
say to Castlereagh that it was unfortunate English
officials were as ignorant of the United States as they
were of South Africa.   He also informed Jefferson
of the incident.   When the diplomatic representatives of two nations found themselves exposed to
such adventures as Monroe met in London and
Merry met at Washington, a careful observer might
easily prophesy that international complications
were not far distant.

[1] Monroe, *Writings*, IV., 150, 158.

CHAPTER XIV

THE *CHESAPEAKE-LEOPARD* AFFAIR

(1801-1807)

THE affair of the *Chesapeake* and *Leopard* occurred in 1807. It was the culmination of a long series of incidents which may as well be treated under this general head. The condition of affairs on the American seaboard and adjacent waters in the years 1801 to 1807 was certainly extraordinary. The people of the United States were divided politically into Federalists and Republicans. The former were especially strong in the north, the latter were predominant in the south. Thomas Barclay came of an old New York family whose members generally espoused the royal side in the Revolutionary War. He had served in a loyalist regiment, and at the close of the contest went into exile. He returned to New York in 1801 as British consul-general, and remained there until the outbreak of the War of 1812. He may be described as standing next to the British minister at Washington in official station, as representing the interest of Great Britain in the United States. He was behind the scenes, was in intimate official relations with the minister at Washington, with the admiral at Halifax in command on the Atlantic station, and was the confidential adviser of the captains of successive British vessels which appeared in the lower New York Bay. His American birth and family connections gave him great opportunities in a social and business way. His correspondence, which has been recently printed, consists of official letters which the writer could never have expected would be printed. They contain many interesting statements, and compel a revision of many pages of historical works which were printed before their appearance.

The mercantile class in New York, as well as in New England, in those days was warmly attached to British interests, both on sentimental grounds and on those of business.[1] The seafaring population and the bulk of the people of New York, on the other hand, were extremely hostile to Great Britain and her officials. The coasts of the United States were infested by ships of war and privateers, both British and French. When the British were in force on the coast the French held aloof, but no sooner were British ships withdrawn than the French reappeared. They seem to have made prizes impartially; but the British having the greater force, and watching the coasts for the longer periods of time, made the most captures, impressed the most seamen, and won the greatest amount of hatred.

[1] *Barclay Correspondence*, 119.

In their misdeeds they were heartily aided and abetted by the judges of the English West Indian prize courts. Rufus King, American minister to England in 1800, complained to the English government of the action of these officials. At about the same time Barclay wrote a strong letter of remonstrance to the home government, in which he said that these judges condemned practically every American vessel that was brought before them, although if the same cases had been adjudicated before Sir William Scott they would have been set free.[1] In one case the vice-admiralty court at Nassau gave a decision in flat contradiction to that of the English admiralty judge. The American owners protested, and on report of the advocate-general the vessel was released in conformity with Scott's decisions. The British government at this juncture took up the matter and reorganized the prize courts. They greatly reduced the number of the judges, provided them with increased salaries, but do not seem to have greatly bettered matters. The interests of the captors and of the judges were practically the same, so that they all worked together to despoil the Americans.

Soon after the renewal of the war, in 1803, an English frigate commanded by Captain Cockburn, who afterwards attained notoriety by setting fire to the public buildings at Washington, was in New York having her decks calked by an American

[1] *Barclay Correspondence*, 120.

mechanic. Acting upon his advice, eight men deserted from the ship. Cockburn at first was inclined to hang the offending artisan at the yard-arm, but wiser counsels prevailed and he was set on shore.[1] The next year, 1804, two French frigates sailed into New York harbor, partly, perhaps, in quest of Jerome Bonaparte, who had recently married the beautiful Miss Patterson, of Baltimore, and was seeking to regain the shores of France with his bride. Close upon their heels came the British ships *Cambrian* and *Driver*, which were joined ere long by the *Leander*. The commander of the *Cambrian* and the senior officer of the squadron was Captain Bradley. He had slight knowledge of international law, and possessed great contempt for the United States and the American people. He brought his vessels inside the harbor and anchored altogether too near the French ships. While there an English vessel, the *Pitt*, arrived and anchored at quarantine. Captain Bradley at once sent a press gang aboard and took eighteen seamen from the vessel's deck as she lay in New York Harbor, and by force refused to permit the American revenue officers to board the vessel until his men were through with their nefarious work. They carried their victims to the *Cambrian* and Captain Bradley refused to give them up.[2] The utmost that the revenue officials could do was to refuse to perform their functions, without which the vessel

[1] *Barclay Correspondence*, 153. [2] *Ibid.*, 167.

could not discharge her cargo. In the end, however, they were obliged to give way, as their action bore most heavily upon parties who were innocent of all connection with this outrage.

For weeks and months the *Cambrian* and one or both of her consorts lay outside of Sandy Hook, stopping vessels and impressing seamen from their decks. Every now and then, when in need of water or when an easterly storm was about to break, they would run inside of Sandy Hook and enjoy the hospitality of the country whose rights they outraged. At length the French frigates escaped through Hell Gate and Long Island Sound ; for permitting this, Bradley was relieved of his command.[1] The *Cambrian* and her consorts sailed away, and from that time on British vessels occasionally anchored off Sandy Hook to receive letters and orders, and also to take on board considerable sums of specie which the United States paid to England in these years, in settlement of the long-standing dispute over British debts which had been contracted before the outbreak of the Revolutionary War. There was no such continuous blockade of New York as has been described by Adams and McMaster.

Before sailing, the French frigates had enlisted seamen in the streets of New York, although prob-

---

[1] Lord Harrowby told Monroe in 1804 that Bradley was removed on account of the *Pitt* incident, Monroe, *Writings*, IV., 247. At all events, Bradley was soon given a better command.

ably without using physical persuasion. There are instances, however, of French officers impressing French seamen from American merchant - ships, as appears by a letter which the French admiral Willaumez wrote to General Turreau, Napoleon's representative at Washington. The letter is dated on board the *Foudroyant* at Havana, October, 1806.[1] Willaumez states that he has just apprehended four deserters whom he found on board an American brig, and suggests that the French minister should make the American government " pay down a compensation for this misconduct in seducing thus our seamen." In the same year the officers of another French frigate seized certain seamen at or near Annapolis on the ground that they were deserters from the French naval service.[2] The truth in the matter of impressment seems to be that all maritime nations, even the United States, impressed seamen,[3] but that the British did it on so great a scale as almost to hide the doings of other nations. Before closing this branch of the subject, it is only fair to say that Barclay interceded many times to secure the release of American native-born citizens who had been impressed on British men-of-war, and that Sir Andrew Mitchell, the English commander-in-chief at Halifax, seems to

[1] Printed in *Peace without Dishonour, by a Yankee Farmer* (John Lowell), 21 *n.*
[2] *Columbian Centinel*, December 23, 1807.
[3] *Report of Meeting at Marsh's Tavern, Dedham, Mass.*, 3.

have released them without demur. The British government also undoubtedly desired to put an end to what it termed "irregularities" and to restore American seamen to their native land. It directed its officers to observe the utmost lenity in visiting ships on the high seas and to abstain from impressments in the ports of the United States. Congress, on its part, authorized the president to interdict at will the ports of the United States to all or any armed vessels of a foreign nation, and to cause to be arrested by the proper official any naval officer who violated the peace of the United States.

In the spring of 1806 the *Leander* was again off the mouth of New York harbor, whither she had come to secure water and provisions. For this object she had sent officers and boats up to the city.[1] While awaiting their return her captain thought that he might as well search vessels going in and out, secure as many seamen as he could, and, perchance, capture a cargo or two. One of the shots which were fired across the bows of the passing ships went far beyond its object, and, striking a wave, ricocheted over the stern of an American sloop which was scarcely a quarter of a mile from the beach. In its course it killed the man at the helm. His name was John Pierce. His body was brought up to the city, and a tremendous excitement was the

---

[1] This incident is admirably described in *Barclay Correspondence*, 230–243; see also Basil Hall, *Fragments of Voyages and Travels* (Phila. ed., 1831), I., 135, 140.

result. The British officers who had come ashore for supplies were forced to hide themselves from the fury of the mob, and the consul-general felt unsafe in his house. Meetings were held, resolutions were adopted, and the provision boats were detained. In fact, no communication was permitted with the frigate. Meantime, Captain Whitby was entirely ignorant of what had taken place. He was anxious to continue his cruise, and demanded the return of his officers and men, but it was some time before the officers could secure a boat and seamen to take them down. Jefferson issued a proclamation ordering the *Leander* to leave the waters of the United States, and forbidding all persons to furnish her with food and other supplies.

The outrages which have been described in the preceding paragraphs were bad enough, but the worst was still to come. British seamen not only enlisted on board American merchant - men; in a few instances, but not in many, they fled from British men-of-war and enlisted on American national ships. The government was alive to the impolicy of permitting American men-of-war to be places of refuge for deserters from the British naval service, and forbade its officers to receive them. It was not an easy matter to determine whether an applicant was a deserter from an English war-ship or was what one might call a private British seaman. In the opening months of 1807 several French frigates came into the Chesapeake seeking refuge after a gale which had battered them severely and had driven one of their number, the *Impétueux*, on the Virginia beach, where she was destroyed by the British.[1] Wherever there were French ships, English vessels were certain to be not far away. In this case an English squadron had the assurance to anchor within the capes of the Chesapeake, in Lynnhaven Bay, and blockade the inferior and shattered French men - of - war. The English ships had hardly anchored when the usual difficulties began. At length, on March 7, a boat's crew escaped to Norfolk from the sloop-of-war *Halifax;* among them was a seaman named Jenkin Ratford.

At that time the United States frigate *Chesapeake* was fitting out at the Washington navy-yard for a cruise to the Mediterranean. She was already four months behind time, and the last preparations were made in great haste. She dropped down the Potomac and proceeded to Norfolk, or rather to Portsmouth, where she took on board her heavy guns and stores, in order to sail for her station. Desertions from the British blockading squadron had been so annoying that the matter was brought to the attention of Mr. Merry and by him laid before the government. At the time it was rumored that these deserters had enlisted on the *Chesapeake.* The secretary of the navy inquired into the matter and found that there were three deserters from

Madison to George Rose, March 5, 1808.

one of the British vessels, the *Melampus*, in the
crew of the American frigate, but that they were
all three of them native Americans.[1] Unknown to
the secretary and the officers of the ship itself,
Jenkin Ratford had enlisted on the *Chesapeake* under the name of Wilson.

George Cranfield Berkeley was now in command
on the American station, with headquarters at Halifax. He determined to take matters into his own
hands. Without orders from England, and without knowledge of the attitude of the United States
government, he issued a circular order to the captains of the ships on the Atlantic station, in which he
stated that British seamen had deserted from English war-ships while lying at anchor in the Chesapeake, had enlisted on board the United States frigate
Chesapeake, had insulted their former officers, and
that the magistrates and naval officers had refused
to give them up. For these reasons he directed the
captains of the ships under his command, on meeting the *Chesapeake* at sea, to search her for the deserters, and, in case a similar demand should be
made by the American, that they should permit
their ships likewise to be searched for deserters
from the American service. On June 21 the *Leopard*
sailed into Lynnhaven Bay with this missive. On
the afternoon of that day the *Chesapeake* dropped
down from Portsmouth to Hampton Roads, pre-

----

[1] See documents transmitted by Monroe to Canning, September 17, 807.

paratory to sailing the next morning for the Mediterranean.

On the morning of June 22 the *Chesapeake* weighed anchor and proceeded on her voyage.[1]   At about the same time the *Leopard* also got under way and stood out to sea.   The two vessels slowly drew together until the *Leopard* ranged alongside the *Chesapeake*, fired a gun, and on being hailed replied that she had despatches.   In those days of difficult communication it was customary for the ships of one nation to carry the despatches for vessels of other nations as a matter of comity.   There was nothing unusual, therefore, in the action of the *Leopard*.   When the British officers came on board, however, the only despatches which he presented were this order from Admiral Berkeley and a note from Captain Humphreys of the *Leopard*.   Barron received the communication at about four o'clock in the afternoon. After some consideration he returned an answer that he knew of no such men as were described in Berkeley's order, and could not permit his crew to be mustered by any other than their own officers. He added that he wished to preserve harmony, and hoped that this answer would "prove satisfactory."

Captain Humphreys did not need an invitation to attack; as the *Leopard* surged along it was observed that the tompions were out of the muzzles

[1] See *Proceedings of the General Court-Martial convened for the Trial of Commodore James Barron, Captain Charles Gordon . . ., of the U. S. S. Chesapeake . . .*, 1808.

of her guns. Unfortunately, the men of the *Chesapeake* had not been called to quarters, as the regulations demanded, upon the approach of the other ship. Barron strove to gain time to enable the men to clear away the guns, but Humphreys would not give it. Three broadsides he fired into the unresisting American, when in sheer desperation one of the *Chesapeake's* officers carried a live coal from the ship's galley and fired one gun. The flag was then hauled down. The British came on board, mustered her crew, found the three deserters from the *Melampus*, who were American citizens, and, as they were on the point of giving up, discovered Jenkin Ratford, *alias* Wilson, in an out-of-the-way hole. Captain Humphreys refused to accept the surrender of the *Chesapeake*. As if to add insult to injury, he returned to Lynnhaven Bay—again trespassing on the hospitality of the United States. The next morning the *Chesapeake* drifted rather than sailed back to Hampton Roads. Barron was tried by court-martial and condemned to suspension for five years without pay, on the ground that he failed in duty in not preparing for action instantly on reading Captain Berkeley's order.[1]

The excitement of the moment knew no bounds; it seemed as if the American people had at last be-

[1] More than two months later a party from the British ship *Columbine* searched a United States revenue-cutter for a deserter within the jurisdiction of the United States at Sandy Hook. See *Barclay Correspondence*, 270, and McMaster, *United States*, III., 267.

come conscious of their oneness. The people of Norfolk and Hampton were especially vehement, for the killed and the wounded by British guns came before their eyes. They stopped supplying the British vessels with food and water, adopted hostile resolutions, and captured a boatload of water-casks. Jefferson was more moderate. It was not until July 2 that he issued a proclamation[1] calculated to abate the excitement, and at the same time requiring all British war - ships to leave American waters, forbidding intercourse with them, and prohibiting supplies to be furnished them. He summoned a special session of Congress, but at the same time postponed its meeting for so long a time that before the members met passions would have an opportunity to cool. Jefferson wished to postpone war as long as possible, if not forever, and to try what could be done by diplomatic efforts. The prohibition of American seaports to British national vessels gave great offence to the government of that country. Canning told Pinkney that it was in effect giving French ships the right to use American ports as a basis of attack on English merchant-shipping.[2] In confirmation of this view it is interesting to note that Mr. Jefferson counted on the French ship *Cybêle* as one of the defences of Norfolk.[3]

[1] Jefferson, *Writings* (Ford's ed.), IX., 89.
[2] Pinkney to Madison, January 23, 1809, in Wheaton, *William Pinkney*, 420.
[3] See, for instance, Jefferson, *Writings* (Ford's ed.), IX., 101.

CHAPTER XV

THE BELLIGERENTS AND NEUTRAL COMMERCE
(1801–1807)

THE French and the English, in the earlier part of their great contest for universal dominion, seem to have been more or less anxious to secure the good-will of the United States; they entered upon the second part of that conflict with very different ideas, and vied with each other to put an end to the prosperity of the neutrals. Students have spent a vast amount of time, and apparently have experienced keen enjoyment, in proving to their own satisfaction that either England or France struck the first blow; but it seems very difficult to ascertain which of the offending belligerents set the evil example.

As far back as 1789[1] the English government ordered the detention of all ships laden with the produce of any French colony or conveying supplies to such colony. In 1792 the French government

---

[1] The orders, decrees, acts of Parliament, etc., are given in Madison's *Report* of December 21, 1808, and printed in *Am. State Paps., Foreign*, III., 262; cf. Bassett, *Federalist System* (*Am. Nation*, XI.), chap. viii.; and in many other places.

declared the ports of that country closed to all commerce, and in March of the next year England and Russia agreed to shut their ports to French ships, and to stop the exportation of military and naval stores and food to her coasts. Two months later France declared that enemy's property on neutral ships was good prize. And so the contest went on, constantly widening with the enlargement of the horizon of the conflict.

With the renewed outbreak of war in 1803 the subject of the relations of belligerents and neutrals again came to the front. Before long the battles of Austerlitz and Jena and Trafalgar made Napoleon supreme in western Europe and gave the dominion of the sea to the navy of Great Britain. From this time on the contending parties strove to injure each other by destroying the neutral carrying-trade, by which alone some of the necessaries of life could reach their opponent's ports.

The new policy began in 1804–1805, when Parliament established certain free ports in the English West Indies to which the enemy's vessels might come with the produce of the enemy's colonies, and from which they could take English merchandise on the return voyage; while at the same time the importation of West Indian products into England from the French and Spanish islands was permitted. The object of this and other measures was to break up the neutral trade with the French and Spanish American colonies, and to absorb its profits as far as possible into English hands.　In July, 1805, Sir William Scott intervened, and gave a decision in the case of the *Essex* which operated greatly to diminish the comparative freedom of trade between the French and Spanish West Indies and the mother-countries in American ships by way of America. In the cases of the *Immanuel* and the *Polly*, he had laid down the general principle that this trade could be permitted notwithstanding the Rule of War of 1756, provided the voyage between the colony and the mother-country was broken by the landing of the goods in the United States and passing through the American custom-house.　In the case of the *Essex*,[1] Sir William Scott stated that in deciding as to whether the voyage had been broken, the question of the intention of the shippers of the cargo must be examined.　If the intention were to carry the cargo from the mother-country to the colony, or vice versa, it made no difference whether it were landed in a neutral port or whether the custom-house formalities were satisfied, or, indeed, whether, as in this case, the vessel was thoroughly repaired in the neutral port; if the intention were to carry on a trade that was forbidden in time of peace the cargo was good prize.[2]　If this decision were adhered to and were followed as to other ships and

---

[1] Robinson, *Admiralty Reports*, V., 365.
[2] See Madison, *An Examination of the British Doctrine* (1806); *The Embargo Laws, with a Message from the President* (1809), gives in full the orders, decrees, and other matter.

their cargoes, a severe blow would be dealt to the American carrying - trade. Ample evidence was given in later decisions that this principle was to be followed. In 1806, Charles James Fox came into office on the death of Pitt and dealt a blow at what remained of this commerce by declaring a blockade of the coast of the continent from the river Elbe to Brest. This blockade was to be enforced strictly between Ostend and Havre, but would not be enforced as against vessels pursuing an otherwise lawful trade as to the remainder of the coast.

Napoleon's answer to this policy was to issue the Berlin Decree (November, 1806), declaring the British Isles to be in a state of blockade, and prohibiting all trade and communication with Great Britain. It is true that the French flag was practically driven from the ocean; but Napoleon doubtless felt that if the English could in one breath declare a blockade and say that they did not intend to enforce it, he might declare a blockade which he and every one else knew that he could not enforce. January 10, 1807, the British government replied with an order in council. This prohibited the coasting - trade along European shores so far as they were under the control of France, which was to be determined by the fact whether or not British vessels could trade to them. Ships proceeding from one such port to another were to be warned by British vessels not to proceed on their voyage. November 11 of the same year came another order

in council; this provided that all ports from which
the British flag was excluded should be regarded as if
actually blockaded by British ships. Furthermore,
it declared that all trade in articles produced by
such blockaded countries should be treated as un-
lawful. On the same day a third order in council
provided that vessels which were warned under the
two preceding orders should be permitted to proceed to some open port upon payment of certain
"transit duties" to the British government. One
month later Napoleon replied to these orders by
issuing the Milan Decree, by which every ship which
should submit to English search or should be on the
way to England or should pay any English tax should
be looked upon as denationalized and English, and
therefore to be good prize.

In reviewing the history of these orders and of
the enforcement of them, the student finds himself uncertain as to how to apportion praise and
blame. On the one hand, the two contending parties
had come to a stand; Napoleon, with France and
a large part of the continent behind him, would
suffer for none of the necessaries of life, notwithstanding the destruction of neutral commerce. Great
Britain, with the countries of the sea to draw from,
could live independently of Europe. A few commodities like sugar and rice, which were products
of non-European countries, would be of value to
Frenchmen and their allies, and could be paid for
in the manufactured commodities of Europe. Eng-

land was in a measure dependent upon the outer
world for her food supply, and keen distress would
arise if the surplus products of her factories could
not be sold. From this point of view, one may say
that both parties were justified in seeking to distress their enemies by cutting off neutral trade,
although, of course, some hardship, if not the greater hardship, would be inflicted upon the neutral.
As a war measure, the acts of either might be justified.

As to the form of the orders and decrees, the intention of the English government appears to have
been to treat the neutral fairly, to give him ample
warning, and to mitigate his losses by permitting
him to seek another destination for his cargo. The
French administration of the decrees was peculiarly
harsh and unjust. Take the case of the ship *Victory*, for example, which was confiscated by the
French because she had been carried into an English port by a privateer and had then been allowed
to proceed on her voyage. Moreover, many vessels
were condemned for having been spoken by an
English ship before the passage of the French decree. An aggravating circumstance in some of
these cases was that the American ship was captured by French or Spanish privateers while actually entering a French or Spanish port. In short,
the French seem to have acted with the least consideration for the rights of neutrals, but the English confiscated so many more neutral vessels, owing

to the activity and strength of their cruisers and privateers, that the greater amount of hostility was aroused against the British.[1]

To this policy of commercial aggression, from which the United States was first of all the principal sufferer, Jefferson and Madison and the Republican party replied by a policy of commercial restriction, which was replying to the British orders and the French decrees in their own mode. Who is to be held responsible for this is not entirely clear. Years before, Jefferson had argued that wars were unnecessary, and that nations could be coerced by appeals to their pockets as well as by appeals to military disaster. He proposed to use the commerce of a country to bring prosperity or business reverses to such foreign nations as would not listen to the voice of reason, and to balance, first on the one side, and then on the other. Jefferson had a physical dislike for war, and he drew largely upon his experience. Before the American Revolution he had seen how potent a weapon was commercial restriction; in the Revolutionary War he had been brought face to face with the misery which follows on the train of armies. Undoubtedly, misery would also come from commercial restriction, but to Jef-

---

[1] For the American view of the case, see *Memorials of the Merchants of Boston, Philadelphia, and Baltimore* (January, February, 1806), and a "Report of the Secretary of State respecting the 'New Principles' interpolated into the Law of Nations," which is printed under this title; see also Madison, *Report on Foreign Affairs*, December 21, 1808, *Am. State Paps., Foreign*, III., 262.

ferson's mind it would not be nearly as great nor as demoralizing as that which inevitably accompanied war. Moreover, at one time, Jefferson undoubtedly thought that to put an end to, let us say, three-quarters of the commerce of the United States would be a blessing, albeit somewhat in disguise. For he held that agriculture was the highest pursuit, and that everything which drew man away from the soil was certain to lead to degeneration. In general, it may be said that this view was held by the Virginia school, by men like James Madison and John Randolph of Roanoke. The actual formulation of the policy of commercial war, if such a phrase is applicable, was due in part at this time to Madison, who seems to have believed in its efficacy fully as much as did Jefferson. He furbished up the old arguments and set forth in print the advantage of such a policy.

In the winter of 1805–1806, when the policy of England—as enunciated by Sir William Scott, and by the destruction of a great portion of the West Indian trade—was apparent, the whole matter came up in Congress. After a lively debate, in which politics had fully as much if not more to do than patriotism, Congress adopted resolutions which had been introduced by Joseph Nicholson, who was in close touch with the administration. These prohibited the importation of such British goods as could be procured elsewhere, or produced in America, such as manufactures of tin, brass, hemp, flax, or silk, of woollen cloth worth above five shillings per yard, of clothing, window glass, pictures, etc. This act is known as Nicholson's Non-importation Act.[1] It did not finally go into effect until December, 1808, at nearly the same time as the embargo.

One result of the peculiar political conditions of the winter of 1805–1806 was that Jefferson was compelled to appoint another envoy to England who should act with Monroe and negotiate a treaty to take the place of the Jay treaty, which the administration held had expired.[2] This he did by sending William Pinkney of Maryland, well armed with a full set of instructions, which directed the negotiators to make a treaty in which the British government should (1) abandon the practice of impressment so far as it related to America; (2) restore the West Indian trade to the footing of 1801; (3) pay an indemnity for captures made under Sir William Scott's decision in the case of the *Essex*. The instructions laid down these things as necessary; as to other points the negotiators were to have discretion. If the British government proved amenable, the abandonment of the Non-importation Act might be promised.

For some years Monroe had been in London, with the exception of the time that he was absent

---

[1] *Laws of the United States*, VIII., 80 (1 Sess. of 9 Cong., chap. xxix.); *U. S. Statutes at Large*, II., 379.

[2] For Jefferson's explanation to Monroe, see Jefferson, *Writings* (Ford's ed.), IX., 178 *n*.

on his fruitless mission to Spain. He had pressed upon successive ministers the desirability of making a new agreement with the United States, and had so far exerted himself in vain. He and Pinkney now approached the British government and began negotiations with amiable noblemen who enjoyed slight power. Before they had proceeded far, Fox died and was replaced by Charles Grey, who in later life won renown as Earl Grey, and was the head of the ministry which carried the first reform act through Parliament. These men were Whigs, but they were completely under the domination of Tory ideas because their political followers were so few in number that the wishes of their Tory colleagues were necessarily followed. After some months' negotiation, the American ministers threw their instructions overboard and found little difficulty in making a treaty (December, 1806).[1] Impressments were not mentioned in the instrument, but the British commissioners signed a note to the effect that the British government would exercise every care not to impress American seamen, and would redress all injuries inflicted while impressing British seamen from American vessels; no indemnity was provided for English spoliations under the *Essex* decision, and, as to the West Indies, trade might be carried on between the colonies of France and Spain, provided the goods should have paid to the United States a duty of not less than two

[1] *Am. State Paps., Foreign*, III., 142, 173.

per cent on colonial goods and one per cent on goods
of France and Spain.   Furthermore, the goods must
be actually American property and not carried on
commission.   Finally, the treaty provided that for
ten years the United States should not discriminate
against British commerce.

The treaty would have saved the West Indian
trade to American ship-owners.   This concession
was so important that Monroe and Pinkney signed
the instrument.[1]   At the last moment, however,
just before they affixed their signatures, the British
commissioners handed them a note [2] to the effect
that the British government would not consider itself
bound by the treaty unless, before ratifications were
exchanged, the American government should give
security that it would resist the enforcement of the
Berlin Decree.   How Monroe and Pinkney could have
signed the treaty after the communication of this
note is one of the mysteries of American history; that
his action did not put a termination to James Monroe's political career is equally hard to understand.

The treaty reached the United States early in
March, 1807.   Congress was then in session, but
Jefferson did not send the document to the Senate
for its consideration.   Instead, he conferred with
his official advisers and some of the senators,[3] and

---

[1] Monroe's justification is in his *Writings*, V., 88, 130–132.

[2] *Am. State Paps., Foreign*, III., 151.

[3] Jefferson's statement of the case is in his *Writings* (Ford's
ed.), IX., 179 *n.;* W. B. Giles to Monroe, in Monroe, *Writings*,
V., 64 *n.*

sent the instrument back to England with the suggestion to the American commissioners that they might use it as the basis for further negotiations. It is not probable that Jefferson expected any good would result from a renewal of negotiations; in fact, he wrote to Monroe that he would better let the matter die gradually and insensibly. He also offered Monroe the position of governor of Orleans territory and advised him to come home. The clouds were gathering; for in January, 1807, while the treaty was on its way to the United States, the English government issued an order in council forbidding the coasting-trade to neutral ships. In one of the last days of June, while the rejected treaty was on its way back to England, the *Leopard* attacked the *Chesapeake*. A Tory ministry had meantime come into power in England; George Canning replaced at the foreign office the more liberal Charles Grey, Lord Howick. For the present the impressment controversy occupied all attention.

The news of the attack upon the *Chesapeake* reached England, by way of Halifax, before the *Revenge*, bearing new instructions from the government at Washington, reached England. Canning at once (July 25, 1807) wrote a friendly letter to Monroe asking him for information and assuring him "that if the British officers should prove to have been culpable, the most prompt and effectual reparation shall be afforded to the Government of

the United States." [1]   This communication was not
in Canning's usual style, and some students have
doubted its sincerity.   On the face of it, however,
there seems to be no reason to suppose that the
British government viewed the transaction in any
other light than that stated by the foreign minister.
Monroe seems to have so regarded the letter.   When
his instructions reached London he found that Jefferson and Madison had seized this opportunity to
endeavor to secure a settlement of the impressment controversy as a whole.   The British government, in the stress of war and with the conservatism
natural to Britons, refused to give up the right of
impressment.   Monroe's instructions were precise.
He declined to abate one jot of the president's demands.   The British government thereupon determined to send a special minister to Washington
to terminate the incident.   Mr. George Rose, son
of a cabinet minister, was the person selected.   He
sailed for the United States in a British war-ship,
and was followed not long afterwards (November,
1807) by Monroe, whose unfortunate diplomatic career thus came to a close.

To Jefferson's mind the British naval ships had
abused the hospitality of the United States, and he
consequently ordered them to leave American territorial limits.   The English government regarded
this in the light of an unfriendly act and stated that

[1] *Am. State Paps.*, *Foreign*, III., 187;   Monroe to Madison, **Monroe**, *Writings*, V., 8.

the American government should have waited before moving in the matter until the authorities at London had had a chance to express their mind on the unpleasant occurrence. The instructions to Rose directed him to secure, first of all, a withdrawal of the president's proclamation. When that was done, he could offer reparation for the injury inflicted. Jefferson refused to act as the British government desired (March, 1808), and Rose returned to England, having accomplished nothing except still further to irritate the people of the United States.[1]

[1] See *Senate Report on Correspondence* . . . *relative to the Attack on the Chesapeake* (April 16, 1808).

CHAPTER XVI

THE EMBARGO

(1807–1808)

AS the conflict deepened and the position of England became critical, whatever lingering respect her rulers had for the laws and usages of nations exerted less and less influence upon their actions. In September, 1807, while the attack on the *Chesapeake* was still the subject of negotiation between the American and British governments, a British naval force seized the fleet of war-ships which the Danes had prepared and which Napoleon seemed to be on the point of confiscating to his own use and behoof. The incident was full of instruction for the American people; its effect was not diminished by the orders in council of November, 1807, which partially operated to confiscate the American merchant marine for the uses of Britain. A month later followed the Milan Decree, by which Napoleon recognized the fact that the orders in council had practically converted neutral merchant-men into British ships.

While England was despoiling American commerce and attacking even her ships of war, the

French authorities had not been backward in the spoiling of the neutrals. When the Berlin Decree was first announced, General Armstrong, the American minister at Paris, had been informed that it would not apply to American ships. This seems to have been only a lure to draw American ship-owners and ship-captains into the maw of French prize courts. The case of the American ship *Horizon*[1] was peculiarly irritating and unjustifiable. She had been captured by an English frigate and taken to England, where her cargo had been confiscated and she herself had been released. She left England for Lisbon with a cargo which was composed in part of English goods, and was wrecked on the coast of France. So much of her cargo as was saved from the wreck was sold for what it would bring. The French courts declared that the money which was received for the English part of it was good prize; the balance was handed over to the captain. Armstrong protested,[2] and was informed that, since America suffered her vessels to be searched by the British, she must submit to the Berlin Decree. The convention of 1800 was evidently no longer binding on France. The Berlin Decree, the Milan Decree, the refusal to respect the convention of 1800, the decision in the *Essex* case, the refusal to abandon impressment, and the orders in council made it imperative for the American government to take some action to protect American ship-

[1] *Am. State Paps., Foreign*, III., 245.   [2] *Ibid.*, II., 805.

owners, American commerce, and American dignity. Great Britain and France might be compared "to a tiger and a shark, each destroying everything that came in their way."[1] The United States might declare war on France or on Great Britain, or on both. This war might be waged by arms and men, or it might be conducted by the silent, and to Jefferson the more efficacious, mode of commercial restriction.

During November and December, 1807, ship after ship reached the United States bringing more and more alarming intelligence. The *Revenge*, returning from France, brought despatches from Armstrong stating the action of the French government in the case of the *Horizon*. This was the proverbial last straw. Jefferson at once sat himself down and wrote a message[2] to Congress suggesting that an embargo should be laid prohibiting the departure of American ships for foreign ports. In the first draught of this document he referred to the orders in council, and declared that "the whole world is thus laid under interdict by these two nations." Was it not better to keep American vessels at home than to send them out with the certainty of loss? As he had no official knowledge of the orders as issued, this sentence was omitted

[1] Macon to Steele, University of North Carolina, *Bulletin*, No. 11, p. 70.

[2] The draught of the message is in Adams, *United States*, IV., 168; the message as sent is in Jefferson, *Writings* (Ford's ed.), IX., 169

from the message in its final form; but the information was doubtless conveyed to Congress in an informal manner. The cabinet was unanimous in recommending this policy to Congress, although Gallatin thought that the embargo should be limited in point of time.[1] On December 18 the message was read in the Senate, which immediately referred it to a committee. The committee reported almost at once. Some senators were for delay, but John Quincy Adams of Massachusetts, son of the ex-president, rejoicing at this sign of vigor on the part of the administration, appealed for instant decision: "The President has recommended the measure on his high responsibility. I would not consider, I would not deliberate; I would act!" The Senate acted on the impulse of the moment;[2] under suspension of the rules, it passed the embargo bill, which had probably been drawn by Jefferson himself, and sent it to the House within five hours after the reading of the president's message.

The House, meantime, had also acted. Upon receiving the president's communication, John Randolph seized the initiative and moved that an embargo should at once be laid; but when the Senate bill arrived it took the place of Randolph's resolution. The next day, however, he took diametrically the opposite tone and declared that the

[1] Gallatin, *Writings* (Adams's ed.), I., 368.
[2] J. Q. Adams, *Diary*, I., 491.

embargo policy was nothing more than truckling
to French orders. The charge thus made by the
erstwhile leader of the Republicans in the House
of Representatives was taken up by the Federalists and served to weaken and divide councils at a
time when all good men should have joined in
defence of whatever policy the government might
have deemed to be best. On December 21 the bill
passed the House by a vote of 82 to 44. In transmitting information of this measure to his government, David M. Erskine, who had succeeded Anthony Merry as British minister at Washington,
wrote to Canning that the embargo was not intended as a measure of hostility, but as a precaution
against confiscation under the Berlin Decree, and
also from the apprehension of retaliatory action
on the part of Great Britain. This latter statement referred to the fact that Jefferson and Madison
had before them copies of English newspapers which
correctly foreshadowed the orders in council of November, 1807. This information Erskine had probably obtained from Madison—wherever obtained, it
probably was correct in so far as it dwelt upon the
effect produced by the decree in the case of the
Horizon and by the statement made to Armstrong
by the French foreign minister.

The embargo act[1] prohibited the sailing of any
vessel from any port of the United States to any

[1] *Laws of the United States*, IX., 7 (Acts of 1 Sess. of 10 Cong.,
chap. v.); *U. S. Statutes at Large*, II., 451.

foreign port, except foreign armed public ships and foreign merchant-vessels in ballast or with such cargo as was actually on board at the time when they were notified of the act. A vessel engaged in the coasting-trade was to give bonds to double the value of its cargo to land the same within the limits of the United States. Discretionary power was given to the president to suspend these restrictions as to any vessels at his will and pleasure. The brief space occupied in passing the act did not prevent considerable evasions of its spirit at the outset by retarding the time when the act should begin to be enforced. Stories were told in the newspapers of the setting-back of clocks and other similar expedients. Many ship-owners preferred to keep their vessels in service and run the risk of loss. This they accomplished by directing their captains, so far as they could reach them, not to enter an American port. Of course, every withdrawal of a ship from the carrying-trade made the profits earned by those which were free so much the greater. Much of this commerce was more or less illegal. It was not long after this time, indeed, that William Gray of Salem, who was reputed to be the richest ship-owner in the country, stated that under the conditions prevailing in Europe an honest ship-master could not carry on his business;[1] the vessels, therefore, of all honest men had better be tied up at the

[1] Gray's declaration gave great joy to the Republicans. See E. J. Harden, *George M. Troup*, 35.

wharves. Nevertheless, the ink was scarcely dry on the signatures to the embargo act before it became necessary to pass a supplementary act requiring coasting and fishing vessels to give bonds to reland their cargoes in the United States (January 8, 1808), under heavy penalties for both owner and master.

The news of the actual issue of the orders in council and of the Milan Decree, coupled with continued evasions of the law, induced Congress to pass a second supplementary act (March 12, 1808), extending the operation of the embargo act to all vessels whether of the size required for registration or smaller. From this time on foreign vessels were to be allowed to prosecute the coasting-trade only on giving bonds not to take their cargo to foreign ports. Fishing-vessels were also included in the scope of the act, and it was extended with a view to the prevention of exportation by land. At the outset there had been some pretence that the object of the embargo was to protect American ships from confiscation by the belligerents. The passage of the second supplementary act[1] made it evident that Jefferson and Madison were expecting to starve their opponents, or one of them at least, into subjection. It was, to use the graphic phrase of Dr. George Logan, transferring the contest from the

[1] For the later supplementary and enforcing acts, see *Laws of the United States*, IX., 10, 69, 117, 145, 184; *U. S. Statutes at Large*, II., 453, 473, 490, 499, 506.

open and honorable field of battle to the "dastardly
attacking the humble cottage, the comforts, the sub-
sistence of unoffending women & children."[1]   Dr.
Logan was an eccentric person, but he seems to have
gone to the kernel of the matter in this instance,
although he was a friend of both Jefferson and
Madison. It is an interesting inquiry whether the
direct attack upon the working-classes of a hostile
country by means of commercial restrictions is ever
an efficacious mode of procedure. Its success, if
such be possible, depends largely upon the country
using it acting as a unit. In 1808 this was very far
from being the case.

From the days of the embargo to the present time
it has been the duty of every student of this epoch in
our history to examine carefully into the question
of whether the embargo could have been enforced,
and of its effects, so far as it had any, upon the
different sections of the United States and upon the
belligerents. It is practically impossible with the
material at present at the disposal of historical
students to come to any conclusion as to the first
branch of this inquiry. It is necessary, however,
to consider the subject with some care in view of
statements which were made at the time and have
been repeated over and over again since those days.
We are told, for example, of ships rotting at the
wharves of Salem and Boston, of grass growing in
the streets of those once-thriving seaports, of the

[1] Logan, *George Logan*, 170.

prostration of the commerce of New York and
Pennsylvania. Moreover, it is often stated that the
ruin of the Virginia aristocracy dates back to embargo days. The truth as to these matters may be
doubtful; it is certain as anything can be that the
ideas conveyed in the assertions just given, and in
many which are substantially similar, have no
foundation in fact, so far as the truth is known or
could be known to any one who made them.

As to the ships rotting at the wharves, the policy
of commercial restriction continued at most for four
years, in which time no self-respecting ship-owner
would permit his ship to rot at the wharf or anywhere else. Moreover, a considerable portion of
New England vessels never tied up at an American
wharf so long as they were likely to be kept there.
The wharves were at no time deserted, judging from
Gallatin's statement that ten million dollars was
collected in duties in the twelve months ending September 30, 1808, six million dollars in the succeeding
twelve months, and twelve million dollars in 1810.[1]
As to the Virginia side of the case, facts and figures
are almost lacking. The conditions of Virginia life
forbade any such supposition as that which even
so calm a writer as Mr. Adams permitted himself to
make. Tobacco was not a perishable commodity
like peaches or pears; it could be kept, when properly cured, for several years. The domestic tobac-

---

[1] Gallatin's report of December 10, 1810, *Am. State Paps.*,
Finance, II., 439.

co market remained open during this time. The great Virginia plantations were practically self-sustaining, so far as the actual necessaries of life were concerned; the slaves had to be clothed and fed whether tobacco and wheat could be sold or not, but they produced, with the exception of the raw material for making their garments, practically all that was essential to their well-being. The money which the Virginia planters received for their staple products was used to purchase articles of luxury— wine for the men, articles of apparel for the women, furnishings for the house, and things of that kind, and to pay the interest on the load of indebtedness which the Virginia aristocracy owed at home and abroad. It is doubtless true, although not susceptible of absolute proof, that Virginia society was already honey-combed with extravagance and debt. Its ruin was already begun; the embargo, so far as it operated to instil ideas of economy into the heads of those whom Josiah Quincy termed the "lordlings of Virginia," was a positive benefit.[1]

As to Pennsylvania and New York, commerce had ceased to be the most important industry of Pennsylvania, for manufacturing had already taken its place. New York, doubtless, suffered from the embargo as much as any seaport of the country;

[1] The revival of the Stay law of 1793 by the Virginia Assembly on February 1, 1808, was in anticipation of hardships to come, and should not be used as evidence of suffering already felt.

but even as to that place there has been gross exaggeration. The truth of the matter seems to be
that the Federalists seized upon this occasion to
place their opponents on the defensive, and succeeded in so doing. The opposition to the embargo in New England was mainly political. The
defence of the embargo in Virginia was mainly political. The strong political contest over the embargo and the successful evasions of the law induced the Republicans in Congress to pass a third
supplementary act extending the operations of the
law to all craft which went on the water, even row-
boats. Collectors were given extraordinary power
to seize vessels and suspicious collections of food-
stuffs and other possible cargoes.

Notwithstanding every effort that the president
could make, it was impossible to enforce the embargo under the existing law. In November, 1808,
almost at the time of the presidential election, Congress went over the subject of commercial warfare
for the fourth time. Those who were opposed to
the administration argued for the abandonment of
the policy. Jefferson's supporters were not united
in its defence, for it was hard to see what effect the
embargo had as yet exerted upon either of the
belligerents. The speeches which were made in the
House and in the Senate had more to do with politics than with the industrial situation. There is
a great deal of assertion in them and very little reference to tangible fact. The debate ended in the

passage of a fifth embargo measure which is known as the enforcing act,[1] as it was drawn "more effectually to enforce the embargo." Under this act the collectors of the several ports and of the stations on the internal boundaries were given despotic power. They were now authorized to seize goods which were "apparently on their way" to any foreign state. Every boat must be laden under the direct inspection of a revenue officer, and the owner must give a bond six times the value of the vessel and cargo to reland her cargo within the United States. Moreover, the collectors at any time could refuse permission to vessels to proceed, and could compel the unloading of the cargo which was actually on board. The enforcing act was drastic in its wording, and Jefferson designed to carry it out with the utmost rigor. He sent a circular letter calling upon the governors of the states where the embargo was constantly evaded to detach bodies of state militia for the purpose of giving the collectors military assistance.

While the country was in the throes of the embargo, the presidential election of 1808 was held.[2] There were three prominent candidates for the succession—James Madison, James Monroe, and George Clinton. Several state legislatures voted addresses to Jefferson asking him to serve for a third term.

[1] *Laws of the United States*, IX., 184 (Acts of 2 Sess. of 10 Cong., chap. v.); *U. S. Statutes at Large*, II., 506.
[2] Adams, *United States*, IV., 285.

After some hesitation, Jefferson replied to these advances that he was old and infirm and also felt that eight years continuance in office of one president was all that the constitution would bear. Successive re-elections would lead to a life tenure, and that, in no long time, to hereditary succession. It is probable that Jefferson was fixed in his resolution to retire at the end of his second term by the growing difficulties of the situation, which could be better met, perhaps, by a younger man; but a feeling that the democratic principle of rotation in office demanded a new candidate undoubtedly had much to do with his decision. Whatever the precise reason may have been, Jefferson's action, following on that of Washington, established the period of eight years as the maximum length for the tenure of the presidential office.

Of the three actual candidates, Clinton undoubtedly felt that the prize was his due—had not John Adams and Thomas Jefferson gone to the White House from the vice-presidential chair? The nomination, however, was practically in the gift of Jefferson, and naturally went to a Virginian. Monroe had for a long time been a political pupil of Jefferson's; but of late years Madison had been in such close official relations that he had the first chance. Besides, Monroe had coquetted with John Randolph and the irreconcilables, and by breaking his instructions had brought his diplomatic career to an unpleasant close, and in so doing had greatly disturbed Jefferson.[1] Under these circumstances, the administration phalanx in Congress rallied to the support of Madison, but even then only eighty-nine of the one hundred and thirty Republican senators and representatives were present at the congressional caucus. Eighty-three of them voted for Madison, while Monroe and Clinton received each three votes. The most interesting person who attended this caucus was John Quincy Adams, who thus definitely threw in his lot with those opposed to the Federalists. Charles C. Pinckney and Rufus King again led such forces as remained to the Federalists.

The Republican party was rent by faction. In New York there were the Clintonians and those who opposed that family connection. The condition of affairs was at its worst in Pennsylvania, where the hostility of William Duane to the administration at Washington and to the governor of his own state, Thomas McKean, had already disrupted the party. In state politics the followers of McKean were known as the Conservative Republicans; they acted in harmony with the Federalists. Duane's hostility to those in power was due to an insatiable desire for offices for himself and his friends. He charged McKean with nepotism, but the evidence presented in the *Aurora* does not bear out the charge.[2] He

[1] Jefferson affected neutrality as between Madison and Monroe. See his letters to Monroe in his *Writings* (Ford's ed.), IX., 176 et seq.

[2] See Buchanan, *Thomas McKean*, 96, for "The Royal Family," reprinted from the *Aurora*.

had thought, with some show of justification, that
the political revolution of 1800 was due primarily to
his electioneering efforts. There is no doubt that
Duane's influence and that of his paper, the *Aurora*, had exerted powerful influence in the campaign.
Duane expected that the patronage of Pennsylvania
would be turned over to him, but this both McKean
and Jefferson refused to do. It was in vain that the
administration gave Duane the contract for supplying paper to the public offices and the job of doing
most of the public printing. It was in vain that
Jefferson told him there were only eight federal
offices in Pennsylvania, that five of these were
filled by Republicans, and that these five were the
best of the eight. Duane had a grievance and refused to be placated. Nevertheless, the Pennsylvania Republicans of all shades of opinion voted
for the Republican electors.

In Virginia there had been quite a rebellion
against Madison, but the malcontents ultimately
went to the polls and voted for the regular ticket.
When the electoral vote was counted, it was found
that Madison had received 122 of the 176; Clinton,
for the vice-presidency, had received nine votes less.
In the congressional elections the Federalists were
more fortunate; when Congress met it was found
that the Republican majority in the House was
seriously diminished. Enough Republicans had
been elected, however, to give the administration a
working majority.

CHAPTER XVII

JEFFERSON'S FAILURE AND FLIGHT
(1808–1809)

THE last months of Jefferson's second administration were the most distressing of his life.
The presidential election settled, the factions within the party renewed their petty contests, and the
voice of opposition to the embargo grew ever louder and louder. The enforcing act which followed
hard on the election did not mend matters much; it
only increased the clamor of the Federalists. Every
collision between the federal officials and those bent
on evasion of the law gave Jefferson's opponents
a chance for vilification and violence which sometimes terminated in riots.

The enforcing act undoubtedly made the carrying out of the embargo policy more complete. At
the same time it gave to Jefferson's opponents greater opportunity for attack. The efforts of the New
England Federalists were redoubled; they denied
the constitutionality of the act; they held meetings in the New England towns and petitioned the
legislature for redress. General Benjamin Lincoln,
collector of the port of Boston, resigned his office

rather than take part in unpopular and illegal acts. The New England Federalists again recurred to the plan of separation which had been talked about in 1804. The majority in the legislature of Massachusetts was now anti-Jeffersonian; they drew up a protest declaring that the enforcement act was unjust, oppressive, and unconstitutional. They issued an address to the people of Massachusetts advising united resistance to the embargo. The condition of affairs in Massachusetts was certainly alarming. Nullification was threatened, and some of the more advanced leaders would have welcomed secession, although it is not probable that any formal steps in that direction were taken. In Connecticut the Federalist leaders sympathized fully with those of Massachusetts, and even went beyond them. Governor Trumbull summoned the legislature of that state and declared in his opening address to them that when Congress had gone beyond its constitutional powers it was the right and duty of the state legislatures "to interpose their protecting shield between the rights and liberties of the people and the assumed power of the general government." This phraseology carries one back to the Virginia and Kentucky Resolutions of 1798. The New England Federalists had come to occupy very nearly the same ground as that which Jefferson and Madison had held ten years before.

It is likely that the possibilities of evil on the part of the opposition party in New England were exaggerated at the time and have been so since. The situation was certainly grave, and the fact was seized upon by the enemies of the embargo to bring about its overthrow. John Quincy Adams, who was now a Jeffersonian, kept the administration informed of what was going on in Massachusetts. It was at this juncture that Joseph Story took his seat in Congress to fill for a few weeks the place left vacant by the death of Jacob Crowninshield. He was convinced that the Massachusetts Federalists were in earnest. To his mind the embargo could not be enforced in New England except at the cost of civil war; an open conflict with England would be better than that.[1] The southern members of Congress were resolutely opposed to war which could only inure to the benefit of New England through the conquest of Canada and the Maritime Provinces. The only alternative seemed to be to repeal the embargo. The administration majority in the House of Representatives broke away from Jefferson and Madison on this issue. The early repeal of the embargo could not be avoided. This did not imply the abandonment of the policy of commercial restriction. In place of the embargo there was substituted non-intercourse with Great Britain and France.[2] This would leave American

---

[1] Jefferson, *Writings* (Ford's ed.), IX., 277; Adams, *United States*, IV., chap. xix.

[2] *Laws of the United States*, IX., 243 (Acts of 2 Sess. of 10 Cong., chap. xxiv.); *U. S. Statutes at Large*, II., 528.

ships free to sail to many ports. It was provided, furthermore, that the president might suspend non-intercourse with whichever nation should first suspend its orders or decrees. On these conditions the embargo was to end March 15, 1809.

Up to this time the Jefferson-Madison policy of war through commercial restriction had certainly not worked well in practice; it had injured the United States and so far had not injured either the French or the English. Napoleon seems to have welcomed the embargo in that it aided his policy of putting an end to the trade of Great Britain. In those days of commercial warfare, ideas of morality and honesty, which usually form the basis of business transactions, were thrown to the winds. Many vessels doubtless carried British licenses, and perhaps sometimes placed themselves under the protection of the British flag, which was quite natural, seeing that they could not enter an American port without being embargoed. At all events, there were many American vessels in French ports. Napoleon issued a decree[1] from Bayonne (April 17, 1808) directing the confiscation of all American vessels which were then in French ports or which should arrive in them. To the remonstrances of the American minister at Paris, the reply was made that under the embargo policy no American vessels could be on the ocean; those which pretended to be American were in reality British. Napoleon

---

[1] *Am. State Paps., Foreign*, III., 291.

regarded himself as merely aiding Jefferson to carry out his embargo policy.

As to England, the case was even worse. The embargo policy was entered upon in an unlucky hour, and was in itself an unfortunate method of commercial restriction. The absence of American vessels from the ocean and the failure to prohibit importations placed a part of the carrying-trade of the United States in English hands. Before 1808 American ships, owing to their comparative immunity from capture, carried on both the export and the import trade of the United States almost exclusively, especially because they could secure freights both ways, and thus charge less for what they carried. Reliable statistics for this period are difficult to procure. The indications are that while the movement of goods from American ports declined about seventy-five per cent. in 1808, as compared with the years immediately preceding, the movement of goods into American ports decreased only one-half, and this in face of the prohibition of the importation of fine goods by Nicholson's act.[1] Moreover, the action of the people of Spain in rebelling against the Napoleonic régime opened Spanish ports, including the Spanish-American colonies, to British ships. At about the same time the Portuguese reigning family removed to Brazil and opened the commerce of that region to Great Britain. It

[1] *Laws of the United States*, VIII., 80 (Acts of 1 Sess. of 9 Cong., chap. xxix.); *U. S. Statutes at Large*, II., 379.

fell out in this way, therefore, that the embargo
proved to be a positive benefit to British ship-
owners and exporters. It doubtless operated to
produce hardships among the working-classes of
Great Britain; the makers of cotton cloth were especially affected by cutting off the greater part of
the supply of American cotton. The ship-masters
and merchants easily made known their gratifica-
tion at the course of events, while the misery of the
working-classes could only become apparent with
considerable slowness.

From the reasons which have been adverted to in
the preceding paragraphs, it may be easily surmised
that when Armstrong at Paris and Pinkney at London, by direction from Washington, called on the
governments to which they were accredited with an
offer to suspend the embargo, provided the other
party would do away with his decrees or orders,
they met with rebuffs, not to say contumely. Armstrong wrote home that the embargo had been over-
rated as a means of coercion. "Here," he wrote,
"it is not felt; and in England . . . it is forgotten." [1]
The suggestion as to repeal which Pinkney made in
due course to the British foreign minister gave
Canning [2] the opportunity to write one of the most
condescending and complaisant epistles in the whole
range of diplomatic correspondence. He stated

---

[1] Armstrong to Madison, August 30, 1808, *Am. State Paps.,
Foreign*, III., 256.
[2] Canning to Pinkney, September 23, 1808, *ibid.*, 231.

that the orders in council could not be rescinded consistently with his majesty's dignity or with the interests of the British people; if the United States incidentally suffered by these retaliatory measures they should seek redress from France. As to the embargo, his majesty did not conceive that he had the right or the pretension to make any complaint of it and he has made none. He would not hesitate to contribute in any manner to restore to the commerce of the United States its wonted activity, and, if it were possible, he would gladly facilitate the removal of the embargo as "a measure of inconvenient restriction upon the American people." With the sarcasm of Canning still rankling in his mind, Thomas Jefferson turned over the government to his successor and retired to the halls of Monticello.[1]

On March 4, 1809, cheered by ten thousand people and escorted by a body of local cavalrymen, James Madison took the oath of office and delivered his inaugural address.[2] He was habited in cloth of American manufacture, made of the wool of merino sheep raised in the United States. In a low tone he read his address, stating in brief that he should follow the general lines of policy which had been laid down by his predecessor. "To cherish peace and friendly intercourse with all nations having

[1] Jefferson left the White House a poorer man than when he entered it. See *Writings* (Ford's ed.), IX., 240–242, 241 *n.*
[2] Richardson, *Messages and Papers*, I., 466.

corresponding dispositions; . . . to prefer in all cases amicable discussion and reasonable accommodation of differences to a decision of them by an appeal to arms; . . . to promote by authorized means improvements friendly to agriculture, to manufactures, and to external as well as internal commerce; . . . to support the Constitution, which is the cement of the Union; . . . to respect the rights and authorities reserved to the states and to the people," these were the principles upon which Madison began his first administration.

In the construction of his cabinet it is certain that Madison at least suggested to Gallatin that he should take the office of secretary of state and that Gallatin would have gladly been relieved of the drudgery of the treasury department. Unfortunately, Gallatin was unpopular with several important factions in the party.[1] The radical Virginians distrusted him; the political clique in Maryland, led by General Samuel Smith and Robert Smith, his brother, more than disliked him; while the "friends of the people" in Pennsylvania, led by William Duane, positively hated him. Under these circumstances the confirmation of Gallatin by the Senate was extremely doubtful, and he continued in control of the treasury department. The position of secretary of state was given to Robert Smith, which proved to be an exceedingly unfortunate appointment, because Robert Smith proved unable to pen

[1] Adams, *United States*, V., 4–8; Adams, *Gallatin*, 408.

the very delicate despatches which it was found necessary to present to successive English ministers within the next few years. Madison, therefore, was obliged to act as his own secretary of state, although Smith signed the letters which were written by his chief. The whole affair was unfortunate, for Robert Smith had made an endurable secretary of the navy, and, as the event fell out, his transfer to the state department failed entirely to secure the hearty co-operation of the Smith faction.

CHAPTER XVIII

INTERNATIONAL COMPLICATIONS

(1809–1810)

FOR some time before the close of Jefferson's administration, Madison had been engaged in negotiations with David M. Erskine, Merry's successor as minister to the United States. He was the son of Lord Chancellor Erskine, was a Whig in politics, and had an American wife. He was out of sympathy with the existing Tory government in England, and was disposed to do everything in his power to bring about an accommodation with the United States. This was disadvantageous in that it induced Erskine to give a false impression to the administration of the friendliness of the British government. In extenuation, it should be said that he was misled by what he understood Gallatin to have said in December, 1808, as to the president-elect's views as to France and to England. We have Gallatin's statements only in the form of Erskine's report; it is certain that he misunderstood or misinterpreted the secretary of the treasury.[1] At

[1] Adams, *United States*, IV., 387; *Am. State Paps.*, *Foreign*, III., 307.

all events, he stated that Gallatin told him Madison disapproved of the embargo policy and had none of the feelings of prejudice against the British which had been felt by Jefferson. He was, on the other hand, an admirer of the British constitution and was well disposed towards that nation.

In the spring of 1809 Erskine received a new set of instructions from Canning. These laid down three points for negotiation from which Erskine was not in any wise to depart. The first related to the *Chesapeake* affair. Erskine was authorized, upon the impartial exclusion of both French and British naval vessels from the waters of the United States, to tender reparation for the attack on the *Chesapeake*. He was not only to disavow Admiral Berkeley's orders, but was to offer to restore the men taken from the American frigate, so far as they were still living, and to make pecuniary provision for the widows and children of the seamen who had been killed, excluding those who were British deserters. In return the Americans were to disavow Captain Barron's retention of British deserters, and engage not to enlist such in the future. If, however, it was thought best, the American government might receive back the men who had been captured, in which case the British government would make suitable provision for the widows and orphans, but no further punishment of Admiral Berkeley could be admitted. The second and third conditions related to the orders in council, which Canning offered to recall provided the United States should repeal its non - importation and non - intercourse acts so far as Great Britain was concerned, while retaining them as to France, should comply with the rule of 1756, and should permit British ships of war to capture American vessels engaged in the prohibited trade with France. Canning furthermore authorized Erskine to make known these conditions to the American government, and if they were acceded to by the Washington administration the king would send a minister to the United States fully empowered to conclude a formal treaty, but Erskine might at once enter into a provisional arrangement.[1]

Erskine did not show the instructions to the American negotiators; he stated some of the conditions, but in such a way as to hide a good deal of their harshness. To this he was doubtless tempted by the conciliatory attitude of the new administration. In defence of his conduct he afterwards stated that he supposed he had the discretion to avoid compliance with the strict letter of the conditions, provided its spirit was complied with in the provisional arrangement. Under these circumstances, negotiations ran rapidly to a happy conclusion. This was embodied in a series of notes [2] which were exchanged between Robert Smith and Mr. Erskine. Acting upon this arrangement, Madi-

[1] *Am. State Paps.. Foreign*, III., 300.
[2] *Ibid.*, 296.

son issued a proclamation[1] renewing intercourse with Great Britain, Erskine having announced that the orders in council of January and November, 1807, would be withdrawn as to the United States on the 10th of the following June (1809). In all the seaports there was now unwonted activity. Cargoes were placed on board the ships which the embargo had caught in port, and they sailed for Europe to anticipate the early revocation of the orders.

Before long, however, doubts began to arise as to the genuineness of the British concessions. In June, while the rejoicing was at its height, news reached America of a new order in council (April 26, 1809) which revoked that of November 11, 1807, but declared the ports of Holland, France, and Italy to be blockaded. Then came news from England that Canning had repudiated Erskine's arrangements,[2] but, with a fairness which should be remembered to his credit, declared that American vessels which had left port, relying on the assurances of Erskine, should be permitted to sail unmolested to their destinations. He recalled Erskine and stated that he would send another minister to the United States to conclude a permanent arrangement.

The new minister, when he appeared, proved to be Francis James Jackson. Canning, in announcing his appointment to Pinkney, stated that he was

---

[1] Richardson, *Messages and Papers*, I., 472.
[2] Adams, *United States*, V., 90, from MSS. in British archives.

"completely attached to all those British principles and doctrines which sometimes give us trouble." And, in truth, he combined in his nature all those things which make the ultra-Britisher unendurable to other men. He was by nature a despot, and these inclinations had not been lessened by his experience at Copenhagen, where he had acted as representative of the British government at the time of the arbitrary seizure of the Danish fleet. His instructions[1] began with what was practically a charge of bad faith against the administration at Washington, and declared that Madison had no reason to complain of the non-ratification of Erskine's unauthorized agreement. The remainder of the instructions provided for an adjustment of the *Chesapeake* affair only after the president should have made a written statement to the effect that Jefferson's denial of hospitality to British naval ships was withdrawn. Then proceeded a long dissertation as to the orders in council and as to what arrangements might be made in regard to their repeal or modification. In short, the appointment of Jackson and the instructions given to him might well have justified a declaration of war against Great Britain the moment they were known. The effect produced by Canning's manœuvres was one of mortification and perplexity. The only clear course which remained open to Madison, Congress

[1] Adams, *United States*, V., 99–105, extracts and abstracts from MSS. in British archives.

not being in session, was to issue a proclamation[1] reviving the Non-intercourse Act against Great Britain, which, of course, did not apply to vessels that had sailed for the United States on the understanding that Erskine's arrangement was in force.

Early in September, Jackson appeared at Washington[2] with a continental wife and a retinue of children and servants prepared for a long stay. That capital city did not impress him favorably; on the contrary, the only comparison which occurred to him at the moment was Hampstead Heath. The president was at his plantation, and Jackson was obliged to wait some weeks before he could be officially received. A typical Englishman, he flushed partridges within some three hundred yards of the Capitol, and spent his time in riding in all directions whenever the weather was cool enough to permit such diversions. His business hours he passed in reading his predecessor's correspondence, which he stigmatized as a mass of folly and stupidity. Erskine, to his mind, had put up with vilification, every third word of which was practically an insult to the British king. In due season Jackson was received by the president in an afternoon frock, himself being militarily attired. He thought Madison "was a rather mean looking little man," and

---

[1] Richardson, *Messages and Papers*, I., 473.
[2] The Jackson mission is admirably described in Adams, *United States*, V., 115-132.

noted that the secretary of state had on a pair of
dusty boots.   A glass of punch with which the cere-
mony concluded reminded him of audiences which
he had had with "most of the sovereigns of Europe," where champagne had been served.   Madison might be a "mean looking little man," but he
soon taught Francis James Jackson a lesson, or
would have taught him one if the British minister
had been capable of learning.[1]   Brushing Robert
Smith gently aside, Madison dealt with Erskine's
successor over the secretary of state's signature.
Gallatin had suggested that the best thing to be
done with the new incumbent was to bring him to the
point at once and send him home, and this Madison
proceeded to do.

Madison began, after the Englishman had had two
interviews with Smith, by writing a letter over the
latter's signature to the effect that further discussions would better be in written form.   This had the
desired result of stirring the tempestuous Jackson
to hint that obloquy would not be patiently borne
by the present British minister.   Jackson wrote a
long letter justifying the disavowal of Erskine, and
stated that when he had left England it was not
known whether Erskine had communicated his instructions to the American government; a perusal
of his predecessor's correspondence had shown him,
however, that the American government was aware

[1] See the correspondence in *Am. State Paps., Foreign*, III.,
308–319.

that Erskine[1] was exceeding his authority. He stated, however, that he was instructed to renew the offer as to the *Chesapeake* affair and was prepared to receive proposals from the president as to the other matters in dispute. Madison replied that only two years before Canning had put an end to oral negotiations with Pinkney on these very subjects,[2] and suggested that the British government owed a frank disclosure of its reasons for the disavowal of its minister's actions. He stated that in presenting the conditions under which he was authorized to negotiate, Erskine appeared to urge them as in the nature of demands which could be receded from, and that he had for the first time learned from Jackson's note that they were absolute restrictions on Erskine's authority. Jackson replied by repeating the charge that Erskine had made known his instructions at the time. To which Madison retorted by requesting Jackson to show his full powers as an indispensable preliminary to further negotiation, and called his attention to the "improper allusions" in his letter implying a knowledge on the part of the American government of the restrictions on Erskine's authority. He further took the opportunity to apprise the Englishman "that such insinuations are inadmissible in the in-

[1] See Erskine's letter of August 14, 1809, stating explicitly that he had not made his instructions known to Madison, *Am. State Paps., Foreign*, III., 315.

[2] See Wheaton, *Life, Writings, and Speeches of William Pinkney*, 407.

tercourse of a foreign minister with a government that understands what it owes to itself."

Before the reception of this note Jackson had written home that Madison was as obstinate as a mule. Undoubtedly, this was true, for Madison, with his simplicity and apparent weakness, was as stubborn as any Englishman, but he also had a good share of the wisdom of the serpent and great experience in the management of public affairs. In rejoinder Jackson stated that he should vindicate the honor and dignity of his majesty's government in the manner that appeared to him best calculated for that purpose. In reply he was informed that no further communications would be received from him. Mrs. Jackson wrote to a friend that her husband had failed, having been accustomed to treat with civilized courts and governments and not with "savage democrats." This last phrase is Mrs. Jackson's, but probably the minister held similar opinions or he could not have written a final note to the secretary of state to the effect that he could not imagine that offence would have been taken at his "statement of facts." He departed for the north, where he found the Federalist leaders were more in accord with his ideas. Josiah Quincy, indeed, averred that the conclusions drawn from Jackson's words were "artificially forced." [1] Jackson himself thought that his conduct deserved full approbation at the hands of the British government,

[1] Quincy, *Josiah Quincy*, 199.

and that they should insist upon his being reinstated. Different ideas prevailed in England, however, and in due course he sailed for home.

General Turreau, the French minister at Washington, had watched with chagrin the course of Erskine's negotiation, the more so because his instructions compelled him to take up an attitude which irritated Madison and other leading men. In the summer of 1809 it seemed that war with France could not be long deferred. Armstrong had communicated the Non-intercourse Act to the French government, and had suggested that suitable concessions from France would be followed by a revocation of that law as regards France.[1] At first Napoleon was inclined to take a high tone as to the United States, but on second thought he decided to make one of those changes of front which have been adverted to several times before. In this decision he was aided by the knowledge of the Erskine agreement and also by a report from his minister of foreign affairs to the effect that the interruption of American commerce had been a cause of loss to the French and had dried up one of their sources of prosperity. On this Napoleon formulated a new decree (June, 1809), which declared that inasmuch as the United States had obtained the revocation of the British orders in council of November, 1807, the Milan decree should be withdrawn. Then came Canning's disavowal of Erskine's arrangement, which

[1] *Am. State Paps., Foreign*, III., 324.

was naturally followed by a second change of front
on the part of the emperor. Another decree (August,
1809), which was never published, provided for the
confiscation of every American ship that should
enter the ports of Spain, France, or Italy, and to
these countries in no long time was added Holland.
To understand the further history of the action of
the belligerents, it will be necessary to recur to the
internal history of the United States.

The inefficiency of Robert Smith became so apparent during the Jackson episode, and the administration was so weakened by the withdrawal of
Jefferson, that it seemed necessary to find support
in some new quarter. The man to whom Madison
naturally turned was James Monroe, his defeated
rival for the Republican nomination. Monroe was
strong with that wing of the Republican party
which had shown a lack of confidence in Madison.
Jefferson acted as mediator and extracted a suggestion from Monroe to the effect that he would accept
the foreign portfolio.[1] For the present Madison
held his hand; the secret of the negotiation was
well kept, and Monroe's acceptance of office, when
the change was made, fairly startled some of those
who looked to him as a convenient instrument with
which to torment the president.

The policy of commercial restriction belonged
fully as much to Madison as to Jefferson. He still
believed in its efficacy, although, perhaps, the best

[1] Monroe, *Writings*, V., 110.

way to operate it had not been discovered. The Non-intercourse Act would expire by limitation early in 1810. Whether it should be continued or what should take its place became the leading subject for debate. Nathaniel Macon, who for a long time had been speaker of the House of Representatives, was succeeded in that office by Joseph B. Varnum of Massachusetts. Macon was now appointed chairman of the House committee on foreign affairs. On December 19, 1809, he reported to the House a bill which had been drawn by Gallatin and had been agreed to by the cabinet, including Robert Smith.[1] The bill continued the impartial exclusion of both British and French national ships, and admitted British and French merchandise only when imported directly from their place of origin in vessels wholly American. The new policy, if adopted, would retaliate upon the British shipping interest by confining the trade between Great Britain and the United States to American ships. The bill passed the House, but in the Senate the Smith faction, joining with the Federalists, amended it by striking out the clause relating to importation. The House insisted upon the original bill, and the measure fell through. A few days later Macon reported another bill from his committee, which is always known as Macon's Bill No. 2, although Macon was not the author of the first bill and was hostile to the second. The latter measure repealed

[1] Adams, *United States*, V., 183.

the Non-intercourse Act of March, 1809, and authorized the president to prohibit commerce with the other nation in case either Great Britain or France should, before March 3, 1810, recede from its policy of war on neutrals. In the House the bill was amended to increase the existing duties to the extent of fifty per cent. on all French and British products. This provision the Senate struck out, and added a clause for the protection of merchant fleets by armed ships. When the bill came back to the House it struck out this clause and reinstated the fifty per cent. additional duty. In the end the bill was passed [1] without either of these disputed clauses, thus re-establishing freedom of commerce until one or the other of the belligerents should withdraw its orders or decrees.

[1] *Laws of the United States*, X., 186 (Acts of 1 Sess. of 11 Cong., chap. xxxix.); *U. S. Statutes at Large*, II., 605.

CHAPTER XIX

MADISON AND THE BELLIGERENTS

(1810–1811)

THE relations between the United States and the warring powers of Europe in the next few years is one of the most puzzling subjects in the whole range of American history. The English government was in the hands of the Tory party, which represented the stubbornness of British resistance to the designs of the despotic Corsican who now ruled France and a large part of western Europe besides. This element was kept in power by George III., and, after his insanity had definitely incapacitated him from ruling, by his son, the prince regent, afterwards George IV. It was supported by two elements in British society: the landholding class, to whom the high price of agricultural products was an advantage, and the shipping interest, which was directly benefited by the restrictions on neutral commerce. The information which came to this government from the United States caused it to believe that the friendliness of the Federalists and of the mercantile interests in the north removed a declaration of war from the range of prac-

tical politics. It was natural that the government
should be misinformed, because its agents in the
United States associated, for the most part, with
sympathizers of Great Britain. This view gave no
weight to the new national feeling which was rapidly rising in the south and in the west, and also
took no account of the changed attitude which
the growth of manufacturing in the north brought
about. The embargo and non - intercourse policy
had diverted capital from its former channels and
had led to an active interest in manufacturing
enterprises, especially in those things for which the
United States had formerly been dependent on
England.

Napoleon was as determined as ever to starve the
British nation into submission by making the people of the continent self-sustaining. To do this he
was willing "to overturn the world." He was willing to risk everything to complete the isolation of
Great Britain, even to making war on Russia itself.
To a mind of Napoleon's abnormal morality there
seemed to be nothing wrong in tricking the American people into a war with England. He hit upon
the idea of seeming to repeal the decrees while con-
tinuing the continental system by means of high
import duties and regulations as to what commodities should be taken away by American vessels.
Of course, it is not intended to assert that Napoleon
thought the matter out at once to its very ending;
but his central idea appears to have been to make

the Americans believe that he had in effect repealed
the decrees as to them, and that it was now their
business to compel the British to rescind the orders
in council or to go to war with them.

Napoleon ordered his foreign minister, the Duc
de Cadore, to inform Armstrong that he could consider the decrees of Berlin and Milan as having no
effect after November 1, following, on condition
that if the British did not withdraw the orders
of 1807 the United States should declare non-intercourse against Great Britain. This instruction
Cadore carried out by declaring to Armstrong[1] that
the Berlin and Milan decrees were revoked, and
that after November 1 they would cease to have
effect, "it being understood that in consequence
of this declaration the English are to revoke their
Orders in Council and renounce the new principles
of blockade," or that the United States, in conformity with the act of May 1, 1810, would cause
their rights to be respected by the English.[2] As
was the case with Canning, so Cadore stated the
benevolent feelings of his master, and informed
Armstrong that Napoleon loved the Americans,
that their prosperity was within the scope of his
policy, and that the "independence of America is
one of the principal titles of glory to France."
This letter was dated August 5, 1810. On the same

---

[1] *Am. State Paps., Foreign*, III., 387.
[2] Cadore's letter was printed in full in the *Moniteur* of August
9, 1810 (XLIII., 866)—in other words, was officially published.

day Napoleon signed a decree[1] condemning American vessels which had arrived in French ports between May 20, 1809, and May 1, 1810. He furthermore provided that American ships arriving before November 1 should be permitted to enter, but not to discharge their cargoes without a license. Napoleon also invented a system of licenses and letters in cipher by which French consuls in the United States should give to American vessels the right to enter French ports.

It seems evident from a consideration of all the facts, only a portion of which were known to the American government, that Napoleon intended to hoodwink Madison and to appear to revoke the decrees while at the same time he did not permit any freedom to American vessels unless the United States should compel the English government to do that which was most unlikely or go to war with Great Britain. Madison fell into the trap. He regarded Cadore's letter to Armstrong as meaning what it seemed to say—that the decrees were revoked—and then proceeded to carry out his part of the business, which was to compel England to revoke her orders by a new appeal to commercial restriction. He therefore issued a proclamation[2] (November 2, 1810) to the effect that commercial intercourse with Great Britain would cease on February 2, 1811.

[1] Gallatin, *Writings* (Adams's ed.), II., 198.
[2] Richardson, *Messages and Papers*, I., 481.

Meantime, William Pinkney, in England, had been striving to bring the English government to a realizing sense of its duty. The Marquess of Wellesley, the elder brother of Arthur Wellesley, who later became Duke of Wellington, was now at the head of the English foreign office. He was friendship itself, but nothing could be obtained from him. To Pinkney's repeated overtures he interposed delays, and when compelled to act did very little. The condition of the government was extremely critical, as the establishment of the regency seemed at the moment to make it certain that the ministry which had been in place would be dismissed. The prince regent, however, continued it in power. When affairs again seemed settled, Pinkney exerted every effort to induce the marquess to rescind the orders and to renounce the principle of Fox's blockade. Wellesley refused to consent to the latter, although he said that the government was ready to repeal the orders as soon as the French decrees should be effectually done away with. Thereupon, Pinkney demanded an audience of leave, and in March, 1811, sailed for the United States. He was soon followed by a new British minister, Mr. Augustus J. Foster.

It was at about this time that Madison made a change in the cabinet which produced more efficiency in the administration and brought to it an accession of power in the person of James Monroe. Ever since 1801 Robert Smith had been a cabinet

officer, as secretary of the navy under Jefferson
and secretary of state under Madison. He was an
agreeable man, with strong family connections in
Maryland and Virginia, but was an endurable secretary of the navy and a wretched secretary of state.
His personal qualities and political power, notwithstanding these disadvantages, kept him in office.
As secretary of the navy he wasted the public money
and was negligent as to his accounts. This brought
him into unpleasant contact with Gallatin, who also
offended the Smith faction in other ways. Gallatin's
power of mind was such, his connection with Jefferson and with Madison was so close, that Smith did
not oppose him in the cabinet meetings, but left it
to his brother, Senator Samuel Smith, and other dis-
contented Republicans to ruin his plans by hostile
action in the Senate. Especially had this been the
case with regard to Macon's Bill No. 1, to which
Smith acquiesced in the cabinet meeting, and his
brother had defeated it by his action in the Senate.
Gallatin also aroused serious opposition in Pennsylvania which Jefferson had not been able to conciliate.

Up to this time Madison had preserved an attitude
of neutrality between the warring factions in his
cabinet and in Congress. Now (March 5, 1811),
however, Gallatin resigned his office, stating that
a perfect heart-felt cordiality among the members
of the administration was necessary. Madison refused to accept his resignation, and authorized him
to sound Monroe as to taking the secretaryship of

state. After consulting with his friends, and conferring with Madison, Monroe accepted the offer.[1] It proved to be difficult to get rid of Smith; it was finally accomplished only at the cost of greatly angering that gentleman. A paper warfare ensued which did not, however, materially help or damage either faction. On April 1, 1811, Monroe took possession of the state department.

In 1809, John Quincy Adams was appointed minister to Russia. Probably no act of the later years of Jefferson's administration was more fortunate than the establishment of the Russian mission, and few persons then in public life were better able to fulfil its duties than the younger Adams. He had been long in the government service, having accompanied his father to Europe in 1778, then being eleven years of age. On reaching that place he began to keep a diary, or journal, which practice he continued, at first spasmodically, to the end of his long and varied career. In transmitting some of the early pages of this record to his "Honored Mamma," he wrote that the journal of a lad of eleven could not "be expected to contain much of Science, Literature, arts, wisdom, or wit, yet it may serve to perpetuate many observations that I may make."[2] A lad who could write thus at so early an age naturally began his active career at the time when most boys are at school. At the age of fourteen

[1] See Monroe, *Writings*, V., 178–185.
[2] Morse, *John Quincy Adams* (*Am. Statesmen Series*), 5.

he accompanied Francis Dana, envoy of the United States to Russia, as his private secretary.

He now returned to the scene of his earliest diplomatic experiences, and was officially received by the czar on October 25, 1809, at almost the precise moment when that potentate had made up his mind to break with Napoleon. The industrial situation in Russia was such that it was imperatively necessary she should have intercourse with the outer world. At this time the Non-intercourse Act operated to send a large number of American ships to the Baltic, which were captured right and left by privateers of countries that were subservient to Napoleon, especially of Denmark. Adams's first work was to ask the Russian government to intervene to secure protection from the Danes. The Russian minister, Count Roumanzoff, replied that he could do nothing, but three days later informed the astonished American that the czar had ordered him to represent to the Danish government his wish that American property should be restored as soon as possible. He had the good-fortune to reach Russia at the psychological moment. It was in vain that Napoleon's representatives threatened; the czar would not prohibit all commerce to his subjects or forbid them to deal with the Americans. On December 19, 1810, he issued an imperial ukase admitting American goods to the empire.[1] In the

---

[1] Adams, *United States*, V., 408–419 (based on MSS. in the state department).

course of the following year Sweden took similar action.

On May 1, 1811, the British frigate *Guerrière* appeared off Sandy Hook and impressed John Deggins, or Digo, a native-born American, from the American brig *Spitfire*. Three days later her officers impressed another American from the sloop *George*. On May 6, Commodore John Rodgers, with the forty-four-gun frigate *President*, which was then lying at Annapolis, was directed to proceed to Sandy Hook to protect American commerce from the interference of British and French cruisers. The tone of this order was something new; it comes down to us across the century as a refreshing change in the attitude of the Washington government. Ten days later the lookout on the *President* espied a ship standing towards that vessel under full sail.[1] Commodore Rodgers supposed that it was the *Guerrière;* he stood towards her to inquire as to the Deggins case. As the *President* neared the stranger, the latter bore away, and it was not until sundown that the American frigate ranged alongside. As the commanders were hailing each other, the stranger fired a shot which took effect in one of the masts of the *President*. The evidence on this point seems to be conclusive. The officers on the quarter-deck

---

[1] The following account is based on the evidence printed in the *Proceedings of a Court of Inquiry Held at the Request of Commodore Rodgers;* Rodgers' report is in *Am. State Paps., Foreign*, III., 497.

heard the report and did not feel the corresponding jar which they would have felt had the gun been discharged from the *President*. The men gathered about the port - holes saw the flash before a gun was discharged from the American ship. A single gun and then broadside after broadside followed from the *President*. In about fifteen minutes the stranger lay helpless under the American frigate's guns. In the morning it was discovered that instead of the *Guerrière* the enemy was the British sloop of war *Little Belt*, a vessel of greatly inferior force. The news of this affair reached Washington a few weeks before the new British minister arrived at the capital. When he suggested that the British government was prepared to redress the injury inflicted by the attack upon the *Chesapeake*, he awakened no responsive echo in Monroe. Commodore Rodgers had redressed that grievance. What the American secretary desired to know was what the English government proposed to do as to the orders in council and Fox's blockade. On those subjects the British minister, unfortunately, had directions to do nothing at all.

CHAPTER XX

APPROACH OF WAR

(1809–1812)

UNDER the conditions which have been described in the preceding chapters, the United States might well have declared war on France or on England or on both, or she might have continued the policy of commercial restrictions. As the event turned out, there would have been no war had Madison remained faithful to his theories, for the disasters to the French arms in Spain and Russia deprived Napoleon of power, and the industrial situation in England necessitated the repeal of the orders in council. It was impossible for Madison, or any one else, to peer into the future and to see things as we see them. At the moment the French government seemed bent on conciliation with America, while the British rulers appeared to be determined to anger the people of the United States.

The British administration caused remonstrance to be made against the action of the American government as to West Florida, and British agents in the northwest supplied the Indians of that region with the necessities of war. General William Henry

Harrison was the governor of Indiana territory, which included the region immediately west of the state of Ohio. He was under the direct authority of the secretary of war, but being a Virginian he often wrote to the president, and also had political aspirations. Jefferson was a philanthropist, but he also had an insatiable desire for land. He wished the nation to grow through the expansion of the section devoted to agriculture, although towards the end of his administration he was more friendly to commerce and to manufactures than he had been in his earlier years, a result due probably to the influence of Albert Gallatin. At all events, Jefferson wished the United States to extend westward, and this could only be done by depriving the Indians of their lands. As long as the natives lived a hunter's life, it required many acres to support one Indian. The only hope for the prolonged existence of the redman in the continued possession of land lay in his ceasing to be a hunter and becoming a farmer. Jefferson, therefore, was anxious to bring the Indians to a point where a small amount of land would suffice for their needs, leaving the great mass of their former possessions open to white occupancy. The Indians, it was well known, were averse to any plan which meant the alienation of their lands. Jefferson, therefore, thought that it would be perfectly fair to lead the Indians into debt, under the pressure of which they might be willing to sell.[1]

[1] Jefferson, *Works* (Congress ed.), IV., 472.

Harrison played his part in the scheme with the result that the tribes living in the region between the Ohio and the White rivers sold their lands. It was at about this time that two Indian brothers, "the Prophet" and Tecumseh, or Thecumthe, whose name is sometimes written Tecumtha, began binding the Indians of the northwest together[1] against any further alienation of the tribal lands, on the ground that the lands belonged to the redmen as a whole, and not to any one tribe. There was a good deal to be said for the position which these brothers assumed, for the alienation of one strip of land invariably meant the killing of all the game for a hundred miles more or less beyond the western limit of the ceded tract. The Indians looked upon the wild animals as sent by the Great Father for their sustenance. They killed them when necessary, but were careful not to drive them away or to destroy them. The whites hunted for the purpose of getting furs to sell. The welfare of the wild animals was no more to them than was the welfare of the redmen. Tecumseh and his brother made a settlement on Tippecanoe Creek at its confluence with the Wabash. There they gathered Indians of various tribes and lived without whiskey. They also cultivated the soil. A group of Indians who refused whiskey was evidently dangerous. Tecumseh and "the Prophet" succeeded marvellously in their design.

In 1809, Harrison secured from the Indians of

[1] Drake, *Life of Tecumseh and of his Brother the Prophet* (1841).

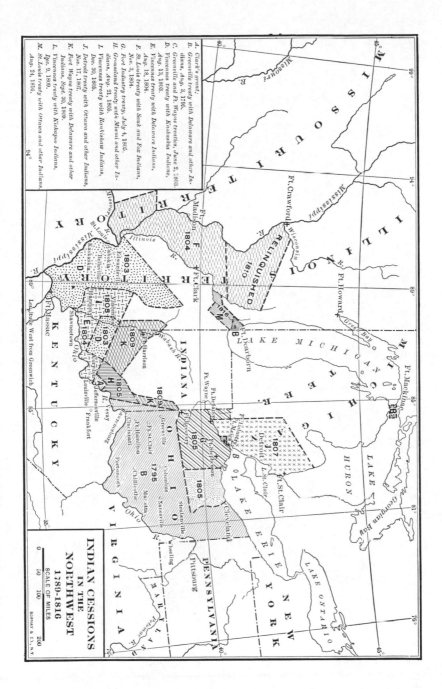

INDIAN CESSIONS IN THE NORTHWEST 1789-1816

southern and southwestern Indiana the title to a
large area of land in the valleys of the Wabash and
the White rivers. This cession included more than
three million acres of the most available land for
Indian purposes in that whole region. Tecumseh
and "the Prophet" stated their case in a most frank
and open way to Governor Harrison. According
to them no Indian tribe, much less any Indian
chief, had the right to sell lands; only the warriors
could decide a matter of so great moment. The
Indians could not live without lands; if their land
was taken from them they must starve or die.
The Indians had no intention of making present
war, but they would resist the occupation of the
Wabash valley at the peril of their' lives. The year
1810 passed without any outbreak; but Harrison
and the government made preparations for battle
with the Indians, which was sure to come sooner or
later. The making of the preparations also hastened
the inevitable attack. The secretary of war, from
the security of Washington, suggested that the best
thing would be to seize Tecumseh and "the Prophet"; but from that time on the orders from Washington constantly varied, so that Harrison must
have been at his wit's end to know exactly what
the government would sanction. In October, 1811,
he received some kind of authorization, but the
letter from the secretary has not been found.[1]

---

[1] See his letter of October 13, 1811, in Adams, *United States*,
VI., 96, from MS. in the war department.

In the summer of 1811 Tecumseh again visited Harrison, and informed him that he was going south to unite the southern Indians as he had united the Indians of the northwest. He seems to have expected that Harrison would remain quiet during his absence, but that commander naturally seized the opportunity of the arch-plotter's being away to occupy the Wabash valley and to pay a visit to Tippecanoe. While encamped near that village, Harrison and his troops were attacked in the night time (November 7, 1811) by the Indians, many were killed and wounded, and there came near being a serious disaster.[1] Eventually, Harrison returned with his wounded to the settled parts of Indiana territory and no Indian war resulted. The fact seems to be that neither Tecumseh nor his British allies were ready for hostilities, and that the attack on the American force at Tippecanoe was against the policy of Tecumseh and the British. Nevertheless, it is difficult to absolve the British from their share in this incident, because it was the arms and ammunition which they had supplied to the Indians that made it possible for them to make head against the whites.

Inciting the Indians to rebellion, impressing American seamen and making them serve on British war-ships, closing the ports of Europe to American commerce, these were the counts in the indictment against the people and government of Great Britain.

[1] Harrison's report is in *Am. State Paps., Indian*, I., 776.

Yet there would have been no war had not other factors come into play. The British still looked upon Americans as provincials who were dependent upon Great Britain for their well-being. They assumed a patronizing tone, which ill - fitted the statesmen of a country which had been forced to concede independence, in saying, for example, that the Americans, generally speaking, "were not a people we should be proud to acknowledge as our relations."

The orders in council had been passed originally to give English ship-owners a chance to regain some of their lost business; but they operated to restrict English exports to the United States. This result came about because of the small exportation from the United States to Great Britain. The adverse balance was made good by the export of commodities to the continent and the payment thence by bills on London. It happened in this way, therefore, that closing the ports of the continent to American trade destroyed American credit in England and put a stop to exportation of English manufactures. The year 1810 saw a great depression in business in England. The year following there was no improvement. The manufacturing industries which were rapidly rising in different parts of England were especially affected by these adverse conditions. These new centres of industry had little political authority in comparison with the ship-owners of London. In the end, however, their distress became so keen that they were compelled to take action and to bring what pressure they could upon the ministry. They presented petition after petition. Each one of these documents inspired the opponents of the government with renewed courage.

In the course of the debates on the orders in council in the House of Commons in the years 1811–1812, the members of the government and those who had generally acted with them found themselves proceeding in different directions. They became confused. While affairs were in this critical condition Spencer Perceval, the British prime-minister, was killed by a lunatic. His death only served as a spur to those who were seeking to bring about a reversal of the policy of the government. June 16, 1812, the ministers announced in the House of Commons that the orders in council would be withdrawn, but the repealing order in council is dated June 23, 1812.[1] On June 18, 1812, the bill declaring war against England received Madison's signature.[2]

Going back a little, it will be necessary to review the action of the English government towards the United States and to strive to find the cause for the hesitancy of its action. In the first place it must be said that the English government was badly served by its representatives at Washington; in all these years it had no first-class man at the centre of

---

[1] Cobbett, *Political Register*, XXI., 815.

[2] *Laws of the United States*, XI., 227 (Acts of 1 Sess. of 12 Cong., chap. cii.); *U. S. Statutes at Large*, II., 755.

American politics. Of the English ministers to
the United States since 1783, Jackson's successor,
Augustus J. Foster, who came immediately after
Pinkney's retirement from London, was the ablest.
Unfortunately, his instructions[1] obliged him to
assume an attitude which was directly opposed to
that which the occasion required. He was instructed to offer reparation for the *Chesapeake* affair,
about which the American people no longer cared,
and not to give way an inch as to neutral rights,
about which the American people were becoming
very much in earnest. Under the conditions of
his instructions, the further requirement that he
should be conciliatory was quite superfluous. The
two survivors of the *Chesapeake* outrage were restored to the deck of that ship, compensation was
made to the families of the victims, and Berkeley's
act was disavowed. But all this made slight impression upon the public mind.

The coming together of the twelfth Congress in
1811 showed that the people of the United States
had at last reached the conclusion that something
decisive must be done. The electors sent seventy
new members, most of whom were chosen in the
expectation that they would insist on a vigorous
policy. They were mostly the young men in whose
hands lay the future of the United States for the
next fifty years. Of these the most prominent at
the moment was Henry Clay, Virginian born, but

[1] Adams, *United States*, VI., 22, MSS. in British archives.

now living in Kentucky. He had served part of a term in the Senate, but this was his first appearance in the House of Representatives. Nevertheless, he was at once chosen speaker of that body. In his hands, by his control of committee appointments, lay the decision as to the policy to be pursued. Another of the new men was John C. Calhoun of South Carolina, who had his reputation to make. He was, at this period, a nationalist, as was Clay. Among the other new members were Felix Grundy, R. M. Johnson, Peter B. Porter, William Lowndes, and Langdon Cheeves, the last two, like Calhoun, South Carolinians. The president's message[1] recounted the wrongs which the country had suffered for so long a time and made various suggestions. The several parts of the message were referred to select committees, at the head of which were the active young spirits above mentioned who had come into political life since the days of the old Republicanism. They belonged to a different generation from the heads of the executive branch. They had all grown up since the time of the federal convention; none of them had borne a part in the conflicts with the Federalists. These new men believed the United States to be a nation and that it should take its place among the nations of the world, making its position respected by force of arms if necessary. By dint of strenuous argumentation, and by the aid of the votes of the Federalists, who sought to

[1] Richardson, *Messages and Papers*, I., 491.

embarrass the administration, the war party carried its policy. It provided for the raising of twenty-five thousand regular soldiers, for the equipping of the existing ships, and for the laying of direct taxes in case war should be declared. The present extraordinary expenses were to be met by a loan, and even the war party could not secure from Congress the power to build new war-ships.[1]

All this seemed warlike enough, and one would have expected that Foster would have advised his principals to look well to themselves or prepare for a new enemy. He was misled, however, into taking a different course by certain Federalists who came to him and explained that they had voted for war measures because they expected that the war would be short, and that, in the end, they could make what they termed a solid peace with Great Britain.[2] How much faith Foster put in this and similar statements is hard to judge from such of his correspondence as has been printed. He seems to have given the administration in England the impression that war was not likely. In taking this attitude he was influenced, no doubt, by the difficulties which Gallatin was finding in carrying on the finance of the country before the war expenses had begun. The non-importation policy seriously diminished the customs revenue; Gallatin's only hope was in the

---

[1] For the details of this legislation, see Babcock, *American Nationality* (*Am. Nation*, XIII.), chaps. iii., iv.

[2] Adams, *United States*, VI., 172, from MSS. in British archives.

loan. But of this only a small portion was subscribed. The reason for the failure of the loan, or for its partial success, lay in the fact that the amount of capital in the country seeking investment was very small. What there was could find ample employment in the new manufacturing enterprises which were being started in New England, in the middle states, and in Virginia. Moreover, the machinery was totally inadequate for laying hold of such capital as there was. The charter of the United States Bank expired by limitation in 1811, and Congress refused to recharter the old bank or to charter a new one. The opposition to a national bank was based partly on the old constitutional grounds which had been put forward by Jefferson at the time of the chartering of the first Bank of the United States. Another reason, it was stated, was that the bank stock was largely held in England, it being a fact that the United States government had disposed of its shares in the old institution to English investors. The most powerful motive, however, which actuated the opponents of the bank was the great dislike which many politicians felt for Albert Gallatin. They desired to drain the resources of the treasury, to embarrass the management of the finances, with a view of forcing Gallatin from office and finding some secretary of the treasury who would be more amenable to their onslaughts on the patronage. The bonus which the United States Bank was willing to pay for a renewal of its privileges would have been exceedingly convenient at this time, and the institution itself would have greatly aided in the floating of a national loan.

Without soldiers and with small possibility of providing any, without a navy and without funds, Foster may well have thought that war was unlikely, and have so informed his superiors. They were also misled by the reports which a man named Henry made as to the discontent which prevailed in New England. Undoubtedly the Federalists, who were especially strong in Connecticut and Massachusetts, were hostile to the policy of the Republican administration. They were accustomed to state their opinions at public meetings and in the public press, and also to talk freely with Englishmen who might happen to stray to New England. All this, however, meant very little, for the Federalist majority in Massachusetts was very narrow. That there was a Federalist majority was due to the fact that the Republicans in a brief moment of triumph had passed laws which went far to overturn the old religio - social system of that state. On questions of national politics alone Massachusetts would probably have gone Republican.

In all the discouraging circumstances which have been detailed above, the war party and Madison did not lose heart. They believed that war was the only remedy for the existing condition of affairs. Once declared, the people would rise, would provide the necessary soldiers, would provide the money.

Madison declared that he would hurl the flag of the country into the ranks of the enemy, certain that the people would follow to rescue it. The existence of this intense feeling in the west, in the south, and, to some extent, in the middle states, was practically unknown to Foster and to the government in England. Otherwise we cannot account for the letters of instruction which Castlereagh wrote to the British minister at Washington on April 10, 1812, and which were the immediate occasion for the declaration of war.

It is true that in one of these Castlereagh stated that England would give up the system of licenses under which British irregular trade to the continent flourished and would enforce a rigorous blockade, thus practically acceding to the American contention that a blockade to be legal must be effective. In the other letter, however, which was itself communicated to the administration at Washington, Castlereagh used language which nullified the force of these concessions. The giving up the irregular trade and establishing a rigorous blockade in effect meant the nullification of the orders in council; but in this other letter Castlereagh stated that Great Britain would not rescind her orders until France, absolutely and unconditionally, as to all neutral nations, withdrew her decrees. To do what America wished and withdraw the orders because the decrees no longer had operation as to America would be "utterly subversive of the most important and indisputable maritime rights of the British empire."

This last sentence was a reiteration of the idea which British ministers had dinned into the ears of James Monroe and William Pinkney. The "indisputable maritime rights" of Great Britain covered a multitude of sins. Affairs seemed to be exactly where they were before Monroe left William Pinkney in possession of the legation at London. Driven to desperation, on June 1, 1812, Madison sent a message[1] to Congress recapitulating for the last time the wrongs which America had suffered at the hands of England and suggesting a declaration of war. After two weeks' debate Congress fell into line and declared war against Great Britain, June 18, 1812. The Jeffersonian system was at an end; a new epoch in the history of the American nation was begun.[2]

[1] *Am. State Paps., Foreign*, III., 405.
[2] For details, see Babcock, *American Nationality* (*Am. Nation*, XIII.), chap. v.; extracts from narratives and discussions in Hart, *Am. Hist. Told by Contemporaries*, III., chap. viii.

CHAPTER XXI

CRITICAL ESSAY ON AUTHORITIES

BIBLIOGRAPHIES

ON the field of this volume one of the most extensive bibliographs is Justin Winsor, *Narrative and Critical History of America* (8 vols., 1884–1889). He prints an extended list of the writings of Jefferson and of the more important characterizations of his career in the critical essay which is appended to Alexander Johnston's chapter on the history of political parties, in volume VII., 294. In the "Notes," which follow this essay, Winsor brings together the titles of the more important books on the lives and writings of the leading anti-Federalists or Republicans (Note B., VII., 315 – 318); in Note E, *Bibliographical Record of the Successive Administrations*, iii., iv. (VII., 336 – 343), he summarizes the sources of information on the subject-matter of the present volume. This mass of bibliographical information includes titles of books which were published before 1888, the year when the volume went to the printer. Its form makes it easy to use; but in scope this part of the work gives the impression of haste in preparation. Specific references are given in Channing and Hart, *Guide to the Study of American History* (1896), 345–352. Bibliographical works go speedily out of date, and this book is no exception to the rule. J. N. Larned, *Literature of American History, a Bibliographical Guide* (1902), gives later titles carefully appraised by competent hands; but the arrangement of the book detracts from its utility as a

topical guide. H. B. Tompkins, *Bibliotheca Jeffersoniana,
a List of Books Written by or Relating to Thomas Jefferson*
(1887), contains titles merely without indication of their
value. Henry Adams, in his *History* (characterized below),
is somewhat scornful of foot-notes; but some parts of the literature are made accessible by the foot-notes to McMaster.

GENERAL SECONDARY WORKS

Henry Adams, *History of the United States of America
during the Administrations of Jefferson and Madison* (9 vols.,
1889–1891), brings together the results of a prolonged
and painstaking research. Mr. Adams is a trained historical student, and had the great good-fortune to use
in the manuscript masses of hitherto unutilized material
drawn from the archives of the United States, Great Britain, France, and Spain. A good portion of that obtained
from the state department at Washington has since been
printed in the recent editions of Jefferson's and Monroe's
writings, and more will doubtless soon be printed in the
new edition of Madison's writings; but the papers drawn
from foreign archives still remain in manuscript. It is
fortunate, therefore, that Mr. Adams was able to print long
extracts from these records in his text. The work thus
takes on the twofold aspect of a collection of sources and
of a secondary authority. The author guides his reader
through the intricate history of this period with unparalleled
ease and at great length. His diffuseness, indeed, is sometimes so great as to befog the points at issue. Unfortunately, also, the author is out of sympathy with actors in
his story and loses few opportunities to sneer at the theories
and performances of Jefferson and Madison, who, whatever
their faults may have been, represented the thoughts and
aspirations of the majority of their countrymen. The
work, therefore, as a whole, fails to satisfy, as it fails to
account for the march of events. It contains, however,
so much that is illuminating and informing in comment
and materials otherwise inaccessible that it must be re-

garded as the greatest contribution to American historical literature in recent years.

John Bach McMaster, *History of the People of the United States* (5 vols. published, 1885–1900). In volumes II. and III. Professor McMaster has brought together a mass of matter drawn to a great extent from classes of material other than those used by Adams. The results of this investigation are presented in detail, but sometimes with a lack of critical insight that detracts from the value of the work to students. The foot-notes are especially useful as a guide and for the quotations from out-of-the-way sources. Richard Hildreth, *The History of the United States* (6 vols., 1851–1852; reprinted from same plates, 1874). The volumes on this period are sometimes cited as V., VI., and sometimes as Second Series, II., III. Hildreth was a careful annalist. His statements of fact are surprisingly accurate, but his comment reflects an extreme Federalist point of view.

James Schouler, *History of the United States under the Constitution* (6 vols., 1880), devotes volume II. to a treatment in thorough sympathy with the aims of Jefferson and Madison, but the body of fact presented is brief and the sympathy sometimes excessive. George Tucker, *History of the United States to the End of the Twenty-Sixth Congress in 1841* (4 vols., 1856–1858), gives a Virginia view of the events treated in this volume; but so much new material has come to light since he wrote that the book has no other interest.

GENERAL COLLECTIONS OF SOURCES

The great collection of materials known as *American State Papers. Documents, Legislative and Executive* (38 vols., 1832–1861), contains a mass of valuable matter on this period. Especially valuable are the volumes on foreign relations. These are sometimes cited as *American State Papers, F. R. F.* They supersede the earlier collection known as *Wait's State Papers*. Taken in connection with the new matter printed in Adams's pages, and the memoirs and writings of actors in those days, they give one an as-

tonishingly complete view. Indeed, the original materials
are so abundant as to almost overwhelm the investigator.
Another interesting series under this general title is that on
Finance (5 vols.), which reprints the remarkable series of
reports from Gallatin's pen. These should be studied in
connection with other documents given in Adams's edition
of Gallatin's writings. The two volumes of *State Papers,
Public Lands,* contain a mass of matter on related topics
which may sometimes be supplemented by turning to the
two volumes entitled *State Papers, Miscellaneous,* and *Commerce and Navigation.* Altogether this series is one of the
most useful contributions which has been made to the
understanding of American history.

The debates in Congress in these years were poorly reported when reported at all. They were collected, so far
as possible, from newspapers and pamphlets and printed
in *Debates and Proceedings in Congress, 1789–1824* (42
vols., 1834–1856). This is generally cited as *Annals of
Congress.* It is incomplete for this period, the debates for
the Senate being sometimes entirely wanting. The Senate
debates were not reported, but accounts of what went
on in that body were frequently printed as were isolated
speeches. T. H. Benton, *Abridgment of the Debates of Congress, 1789–1856* (16 vols., 1857–1861), is useful. The
Journals of the Senate and the House give the opportunity
to follow a bill through its various stages, and the *Executive Journal of the Senate* is exceedingly important for the
study of office-holding. The contemporaneous edition of
the *Laws of the United States, Published by Authority,* is the
one cited in this volume; but I have added the chapter and
statute and also page references to the second volume of
the *Statutes at Large.* The most convenient storehouse for
the messages of the presidents and documents which accom-
pany them is J. D. Richardson, *A Compilation of the Messages and Papers of the Presidents* (10 vols., 1896–1899).
Volume I. contains the messages of Jefferson and Madison.
Professor MacDonald reprints a few documents of this time
in his *Select Documents Illustrative of the History of the United*

States, 1776, 1861 (1901); Albert Bushnell Hart, in the third volume of his *American History Told by Contemporaries*, devotes more space to it, especially extracts from contemporary narrative and correspondence.

THOMAS JEFFERSON

Besides the bibliography of books written by or relating to Jefferson in Tompkins, *Bibliotheca Jeffersoniana*, Paul Leicester Ford has prepared a list of Jefferson's printed works in the Introduction of his edition of Jefferson, *Writings* (I., xxxiv.–xxxvi.).

The Writings of Thomas Jefferson, Collected and Edited by Paul Leicester Ford (10 vols., 1892–1899), is the best edition. Volumes VII.–IX. cover the period 1801–1812. This edition contains many pieces from the MS. *Jefferson Papers*, which were printed in extract in Henry Adams, *United States*. The earlier edition of *The Writings of Thomas Jefferson*, edited by H. A. Washington (9 vols., 1853–1854; reprinted in 1864 and 1884), is still useful, as it contains some matter not in Ford's edition. It is usually cited as the "Congress edition." Both of these publications are made up mainly from that portion of the MS. *Jefferson Papers* which was sold to the government in 1848 by T. J. Randolph. They do not exhaust the Jefferson manuscripts in the state department, as can be seen by comparing them with the *Calendar of the Correspondence of Thomas Jefferson*, printed in the Bureau of Rolls and Library of the Department of State, *Bulletins* (No. 6, "Letters from Jefferson"; No. 8, "Letters to Jefferson"; No. 10, "Supplementary"). Another portion of the *Jefferson Papers* retained by the family in 1848, and containing the less official and private papers, came into the possession of Thomas Jefferson Coolidge and were given by him to the Massachusetts Historical Society. Most of the more valuable papers in this collection, together with others presented by Professor A. C. Coolidge, were printed in the Massachusetts Historical Society, *Collections* (7th

series, I.). Late in life Jefferson culled from his papers
certain memoranda which he regarded as illustrative of his
public career, and put them together under the title of
"Anas." These are printed in Jefferson, *Writings* (Ford's
edition, I.); they have also been printed, with some addi-
tions, as *The Complete Anas of Thomas Jefferson* (1903).
The "Anas" in the period of the present volume contain
many "Notes of discussion in Cabinet," and other matter
which throws an important light upon the inner working of
the administration. S. E. Forman has published *The Life
and Writings of Thomas Jefferson—Including all of His Important Utterances on Public Questions* (1900). The latter
part of this compilation is arranged alphabetically and forms
a useful short cut to the third president's ideas on national
subjects and on the public characters of his time.

Henry S. Randall, *The Life of Thomas Jefferson* (3 vols.,
1858), is still regarded as the standard life of Jefferson,
partly because its author had access to material which no
other writer has used; but it is a very prejudiced book, and
often unfair to Hamilton and the Federalists. Another
work on the Jeffersonian era is George Tucker, *The Life of
Thomas Jefferson* (2 vols., 1837). This work, by the professor of moral philosophy in the University of Virginia,
gives the Virginia view of one of the greatest men of that
state, and contains information from local sources that is
not to be found in northern books. James Parton, *Life of
Thomas Jefferson* (1874), is written in a brilliant manner
and in a sympathetic spirit, but not always according
to the canons of historical criticism. Cornelis de Witt,
*Thomas Jefferson, Étude historique sur la Démocratie Amé-
ricaine* (Paris, 1861 and 1862; also translated into English).
gives the view of a French doctrinaire. Nevertheless, it is
a stimulating and interesting book. Paul Leicester Ford
has analyzed Jefferson's politico - ethical aspirations in
his *Thomas Jefferson* (Elson, *Monographs of the American
Revolution*). Among other works laudatory in tone are
B. L. Rayner, *The Life, Writings, and Opinions of Thomas
Jefferson* (1832); James Schouler, *Thomas Jefferson* (*Mak-*

ers of America series, 1893); and the two books by Thomas
E. Watson, both entitled *Thomas Jefferson* (one in 2 vols.,
1903, the other in *Beacon Biographies*).   Of the works
hostile to Jefferson may be mentioned Theodore Dwight,
*The Character of Thomas Jefferson as Exhibited in His
Own Writings* (1839); [Stephen C. Carpenter] *Memoirs of
the Hon. Thomas Jefferson, . . . with a View of the Rise and
Progress of French Influence and French Principles in This
Country* (1809); and John T. Morse, Jr., *Thomas Jefferson*
(*American Statesmen* series).   Possibly, Henry C. Merwin's
slight study of this great career (*Riverside Biographical
series, No. 5, 1901*) gives a fairer view of Jefferson's life
than any of the larger works.

Jefferson's great-granddaughter, Sarah Nicholas Randolph, has published a book entitled *Domestic Life of Thomas
Jefferson* (1871).   It was compiled from the manuscripts
retained in 1848, and which had not then come into the
possession of the Massachusetts Historical Society, and
from the traditions of the Randolph family.   It has the
failings of family biographical work; but it also has the
merits which attach to undisguised family tradition.   H.
N. Pierson, *Jefferson at Monticello—The Private Life of
Thomas Jefferson* (1862), consists of matter procured by
the compiler from Captain Edmund Bacon, who had acted
as Jefferson's superintendent at Monticello in his last years.
These are the recollections by an old man of earlier association with the retired president.   They possess all the
faults of that class of material, but at the same time admit
the student to a glimpse of Virginia life in the olden time.
L. H. Boutelle, *Thomas Jefferson, the Man of Letters* (Chi-
cago, 1891), is an interesting treatment of a generally neg-
lected side of a highly talented man.

REPUBLICAN LEADERS

There is no adequate life of Madison.   Rives's book
stops with the close of Washington's administration; Gaillard Hunt, *The Life of James Madison* (1902), is written

from the sources, but it is so brief on this portion of Madison's career as to be practically useless. Sidney Howard Gay, *James Madison* (*American Statesmen* series), is even briefer and very unsympathetic. Under these circumstances, John Quincy Adams's eulogistic narrative in his *Lives of James Madison and James Monroe, with Historical Notices of Their Administrations* (1850), remains the best statement as to his services to the United States during the years covered by this volume. The public papers of James Madison were purchased by Congress, but so far little use has been made of them in any formal collection of Madison's writings. The *Letters and Other Writings of James Madison*, published at Philadelphia in 1865, contain some letters covering this period; the new edition of the *Writings of James Madison*, by Gaillard Hunt, will doubtless contain valuable matter on this epoch, but up to 1905 had reached only the year 1790, while the letters in the *Madison Papers* (1840) cease with the year 1787. The state department has published, in Bureau of Rolls and Library, *Bulletin*, No. 4, a *Calendar of the Correspondence of James Madison* (with an index in supplement). The *Memoirs and Letters of Dolly Madison, Edited by Her Grandniece* (1886), contains interesting glimpses of life at Washington in the first part of the nineteenth century.

J. Q. Adams's eulogistic notice of Monroe, cited above, remains the best memoir—in fact, almost the only one of any value Thirty pages sufficed Daniel C. Gilman for his description of this portion of Monroe's life in *James Monroe* (*American Statesmen* series). S. M. Hamilton is now editing the *Writings of Monroe*. Of these, volumes III.-V. cover the years 1801–1812. The chief reliance in this publication has been the *Monroe Papers*, which Congress bought for twenty thousand dollars from Mrs. Monroe after the president's death. Some papers have also been found in other places. It may be noted that the documents printed in Ford's and Hamilton's editions of the writings of Jefferson and Monroe have cleared up a good many hitherto obscure points in the latter's career. The Bureau of Rolls and Library of the state department, *Bulletins*, No. 2, contains a *Calendar of the Correspondence of James Monroe.* In the appendix to Gilman, *Monroe*, there is a "Bibliography of Monroe and the Monroe Doctrine," by J. Franklin Jameson. The career of Albert Gallatin seems to have had peculiar interest for Henry Adams. The eccentricities of Gallatin's character and his way of looking at Jefferson's pet plans arouse a sympathetic chord in Adams's historical being. His *Life of Albert Gallatin* (1879) has none of that acerbity of judgment which make his *History* and his *John Randolph* painful reading to one who admires both Henry Adams's historical method and performance and Thomas Jefferson's desires and struggles for their fulfilment. Adams has also edited the *Writings of Albert Gallatin* (3 vols., 1879). John Austin Stevens, *Albert Gallatin* (*American Statesmen* series), is an excellent brief statement of Gallatin's services. The period covered by the present work is described in two chapters entitled "Secretary of the Treasury" and "In the Cabinet." In the former, Mr. Stevens gives a clear statement of the financial history of the time; in the latter he deals with Gallatin's influence with Jefferson and Madison in other respects. John Randolph of Roanoke, has found two biographers; Henry Adams has written a remarkable study of his grandfather's opponent—remarkable for its scholarly insight and its entire lack of sympathy with the subject (*American Statesmen* series); but Hugh A. Garland, *Life of John Randolph* (1850), remains the principal source of information; it errs as much in the direction of over-sympathy as Adams does in judging a man of Randolph's caliber by the canons of cold historical criticism. William E. Dodd, in his *Life of Nathaniel Macon* (1903), long Randolph's friend and follower, adds little to our knowledge of this part of Macon's career; the student will get more satisfaction from a perusal of Macon's letters in K. P. Battle [ed.], *Letters of Nathaniel Macon, John Steele, and William Barry Grove* (*James Sprunt Historical Monographs*, No. 3), issued by the University of North Carolina, *Bulletins*, No. 11.

THE LOUISIANA PURCHASE

The reports, letters, etc., which passed in the course of this transaction are printed in *American State Papers* (folio edition), *Foreign Relations*, II.; and *Public Lands*, I.; in Jefferson's *Writings*, preferably Ford's edition, VIII.; in Monroe's *Writings*, IV.; in *Annals of Congress*, XII., Appendix. The story is admirably told in Henry Adams, *History of the United States*, I., and in a somewhat different form from about the same materials in F. A. Ogg, *The Opening of the Mississippi* (1904). The French side of the affair was told by Napoleon's representative in a volume intended to justify the sale in the eyes of Frenchmen. The title of this work is Barbé-Marbois, *Histoire de la Louisiane et de la Cession* (1829); and in the English translation as *The History of Louisiana, Particularly of the Cession of That Colony to the United States* (1830). Villiers du Terrage, *Les Dernières Années de la Louisiane Française* (1903), prints some new matter on this topic; but this portion of Louisiana's story is treated very briefly, though on the earlier portion it is the best work that we have. C. E. A. Gayarré, *History of Louisiana* (revised edition, 1885), is generally regarded as the standard history of that portion of the old Louisiana which now forms the state of the same name; it was written before the appearance of Adams's volumes, and before the publication of the documents contained in Villiers du Terrage's important work. Of the minor works on Louisiana may be mentioned the school history of that state by Grace King and J. R. Ficklen; T. M. Cooley, *Acquisition of Louisiana;* C. F. Robertson, *Louisiana Purchase* (American Historical Association, *Papers*); and an article by J. P. Quincy in Massachusetts Historical Society, *Proceedings* (2d series, XVIII.), a very hostile view.

EXPLORATIONS

With the loose ideas as to the proprietorship of public documents which prevailed in those days, the manuscript journals and other materials of the Lewis and Clark expedition and of Pike's exploration were not transmitted to the war department for safe keeping, but remained in private hands, or were deposited with the American Philosophical Society at Philadelphia. No attempt was made to print the original material at the time; the only thought was to dress it up in book form for public perusal. Pike performed this task for himself, and produced a remarkable book, which was first printed in 1810. He had no literary training, and the form and arrangement of his material is sometimes puzzling, but the personality of the explorer and author is so interesting, and the adventures through which he passed were so exciting, that the book not only enjoyed great reputation, but called an undue amount of attention to Pike's expedition in comparison with that of Lewis and Clark, which was far more important and the results of which were vastly more far-reaching. The title of the original edition was Zebulon M. Pike, *Account of Expeditions to the Sources of the Mississippi and through the Western Parts of Louisiana, during the Years 1805, 1806, 1807. And a Tour through the Interior Parts of New Spain* (2 vols., 1810). It has often been reprinted; the standard edition is that of Dr. Elliott Coues (3 vols., 1895). This is not an exact reprint of the original, for Dr. Coues tried to combine Pike's text and his appendices into one continuous narrative, which is copiously illustrated with valuable notes.

Members of the Lewis and Clark expedition from the leaders down kept journals and diaries in considerable profusion. The leaders clearly recognized the desirability of getting this matter before the public in some readable form, but the task proved to be a matter of considerable difficulty. Lewis died mysteriously while on his way to the east, possibly to oversee some such publication, and the matter fell into the hands of Clark, whose time was fully occupied with other business. He therefore employed Nicholas Biddle, of Philadelphia, to select from the manuscripts the significant portions and put them into

literary form. Biddle did his work admirably and produced a book which is a classic, by paraphrasing the language of the explorers and correcting their spelling where
he repeated their words. The final revision and seeing the
book through the press was confided to Paul Allen, whose
name appears on the title-page, and the work is often
cited under his name as Allen's *History of the Expedition of
Lewis and Clark*. The process of editing, which has just
been described, took time, and no less than three printers
were tried before one was found who remained solvent
long enough to publish the book. It fell out, therefore,
that the details of the Lewis and Clark expedition, admirably told by themselves and Nicholas Biddle, did not get
before the public until 1814. The original title is *History
of the Expedition under the Command of Captains Lewis and
Clark to the Sources of the Missouri, thence Across the Rocky
Mountains and down the River Columbia to the Pacific
Ocean, 1804, 1805, 1806. Prepared for the Press by Paul
Allen* (2 vols., 1814). In 1893 Elliott Coues published an
uncritical reprint of this edition with notes, containing
extensive extracts from the original journals and much
biographical and bibliographical information, all contained
in four volumes (*History of the Expedition under the Command of Lewis and Clark; a New Edition*, 1893). In 1904
was begun the publication of a complete edition from the
original journals of Lewis and Clark and other members of
the expedition under the title of *Original Journals of the
Lewis and Clark Expedition, 1804–1806* (1904–——), edited
by Reuben Gold Thwaites. This is a remarkable and unique
production in which one can read different accounts of the
doings of the expedition on a given day from the pens of
different members of the party, all printed with ruthless
accuracy. A few hundred pages of the original language
of these men are interesting on account of its roughness of
expression and disregard of the niceties of spelling, but
most readers would probably prefer the more orderly statement of Nicholas Biddle. There are numerous biographies
and biographical sketches, but an equal amount of reading

of the detailed accounts will convey a better idea of the spirit and heroism of these remarkable men. Jefferson provided a memoir of Lewis for the "Biddle edition," which has been often reprinted.

THE BURR EXPEDITION

Henry Adams, in the third volume of his *History of the United States*, prints long extracts from the archives of Great Britain and Spain relating to the Burr conspiracy. Walter Flavius McCaleb, *The Aaron Burr Conspiracy: a History Largely from Original and Hitherto Unused Sources* (1903), gives the result of research in the depositories of documents in Texas and interesting extracts from western papers and letters of the time. These two publications have practically reconstructed the story of the Burr expeditions and have rendered all earlier accounts to a great extent obsolete. These two authorities disagree in some of their results, but on many points they are in agreement. McCaleb printed a study of his new material in the American Historical Association, *Papers*, 1903, vol. I. Of the older material, see Robertson, *Reports of the Trials of Colonel Aaron Burr for Treason and for a Misdemeanor* (2 vols., 1808); *The Trial of Colonel Aaron Burr* (3 vols., 1807–1808), including the arguments and decisions; J. J. Combs, *Trial of Aaron Burr for High Treason* (1867); there is also much about the trial in Kennedy, *Memoirs of William Wirt* (2 vols., 1849). James Parton, *The Life and Times of Aaron Burr* (1858); M. L. Davis, *Memoirs of Aaron Burr, with Miscellaneous Selections from His Correspondence* (2 vols., 1836–1837); W. H. Safford, *The Blennerhassett Papers; embodying the private Journal of Harman Blennerhassett, and the hitherto unpublished correspondence of Burr, Alston, and others . . . and a Memoir* (1864); and General James Wilkinson, *Memoirs of My Own Times* (3 vols., 1816), are also largely devoted to this topic. Further references may be found in J. Winsor, *Narrative and Critical History of America*, VII., 338–340.

INTERNATIONAL RELATIONS

This topic is treated almost to the exclusion of other matter in volumes IV., V., and VI. of Henry Adams, *History of the United States*, which contain so much hitherto unprinted matter that they may be regarded almost in the light of an original source. In the writings of Jefferson, Madison, Monroe, and Gallatin will be found much valuable illustrative material in addition to that which is printed in the *American State Papers* (folio edition), *Foreign Relations*. Henry Wheaton, *Some Account of the Life, Writings, and Speeches of William Pinkney* (1826), and more especially Rev. William Pinkney, *The Life of William Pinkney* (1853), are convenient as bringing together material, which is largely reprinted elsewhere, on the relations with England in the years 1807 – 1811. Much new material has been brought to light by the publication, under the editorship of George Lockhart Rives, of the *Correspondence of Thomas Barclay* (1894).

In this and the following paragraphs are included some of the more important contemporary pamphlets which have been found useful in the preparation of the preceding account. They are here arranged, for the most part, in chronological order. Any study of this subject should begin with a perusal of two short contemporary treatises, James Stephen, *War in Disguise; or, the Frauds of the Neutral Flags* (1805); and *An Examination of the British Doctrine which Subjects to Capture a Neutral Trade not Open in Time of Peace* (1806). The latter paper was written by James Madison and was intended to place between two covers a recapitulation of British misdeeds up to the time of publication. Like all of Madison's writings, it was well suited to its purpose. The year 1807 was replete with pamphlets on this general theme, among which may be mentioned *A True Picture of the United States of America, being a Brief Statement of the Conduct of the Government and People of that Country towards Great Britain by a British Subject* (1807); this contains some interesting figures and tables. Another tract printed in England in the same year, entitled *Old England and America against France and All Europe*, by Patrioticus, advocated union between England and the United States, which may be said to have been the burden of John Lowell's Federalistic tract entitled *Peace without Dishonor : War without Hope, being a Calm and Dispassionate Enquiry into the Question of the Chesapeake by a Yankee Farmer* (Boston, 1807). In this paper Mr. Lowell attempted to justify the attack on the *Chesapeake* as being in harmony with the rules of international law. Another pamphlet on the same affair is an *Essay on the Rights and Duties of Nations Relative to Fugitives from Justice, Considered with Reference to the Affair of the Chesapeake* (1807). The official correspondence may easily be consulted in the *Report of the (Senate) Committee on Correspondence between Monroe and Canning and Madison and Rose Relative to the Attack on the Chesapeake* (April 16, 1808); with this should be read *Letters from the Secretary of State to Mr. Monroe on the Subject of Impressment*, which also includes extracts from Monroe's letters. Most of this matter has also been printed in the official documents and in the recent editions of the writings of the statesmen of that time, but they are brought together here in a very convenient form. The same thing may be said of W. J. Duane, *The Law of Nations*, which contains (71–73) a chronology of the misdeeds of England and France.

A pamphlet which had nearly as much influence as Stephen, *War in Disguise*, but on the other side, was Alexander Baring, *An Inquiry into the Causes and Consequences of the Orders in Council and an Examination of the Conduct of Great Britain towards the Neutral Commerce of America* (1808). The *Speech of Henry Brougham before the House of Commons in Support of Petitions against the Orders in Council* (1808) supplements this tract. Written from the other point of view is the *Observations on the American Treaty in Eleven Letters by Decius* (1808). This was written by Thomas Peregrine Courtenay, and was a fierce attack from the British point of view on Monroe's rejected treaty, which was as distasteful to some persons in England as it was to Mr. Jefferson.

The English orders, French decrees, and American laws and proclamations restricting commerce, beginning with 1793, may be found in one volume entitled *The Embargo Laws* (1809), to which is added an appendix. The effects of the policy of commercial restrictions may be studied in Gallatin's *Report* of December 10, 1810 (*American State Papers, Finance*). Further information is given in the *Speech of William B. Giles on the Motion of Mr. Hillhouse to Repeal the Embargo Laws* (1808) and in *An Address to the Citizens of Massachusetts on the Causes and Remedy of our National Distresses, by a Fellow-Sufferer* (1808).

INDEX